985
FER

Ferreira, Cesar.

Culture and customs
of Peru.

$44.95

| DATE | | | |
|------|------|------|------|
|  |  |  |  |
|  |  |  |  |
|  |  |  |  |
|  |  |  |  |
|  |  |  |  |
|  |  |  |  |
|  |  |  |  |
|  |  |  |  |
|  |  |  |  |
|  |  |  |  |
|  |  |  |  |
|  |  |  |  |
|  |  |  |  |

BAKER & TAYLOR

# Culture and Customs of Peru

**Recent Titles in**
**Culture and Customs of Latin America and the Caribbean**

Culture and Customs of Argentina
*David William Foster, Melissa Fitch Lockhart, and Darrell B. Lockhart*

Culture and Customs of Colombia
*Raymond Leslie Williams and Kevin G. Guerrieri*

Culture and Customs of the Dominican Republic
*Isabel Z. Brown*

Culture and Customs of Ecuador
*Michael Handelsman*

Culture and Customs of Costa Rica
*Chalene Helmuth*

Culture and Customs of Chile
*Guillermo I. Castillo-Feliú*

Culture and Customs of Guatemala
*Maureen E. Shea*

Culture and Customs of Cuba
*William Luis*

Culture and Customs of Haiti
*J. Michael Dash*

Culture and Customs of Jamaica
*Martin Mordecai and Pamela Mordecai*

Culture and Customs of El Salvador
*Roy C. Boland*

Culture and Customs of Venezuela
*Mark Dinneen*

# Culture and Customs of Peru

∾●∾

## César Ferreira
## and
## Eduardo Dargent-Chamot

Culture and Customs of Latin America
and the Caribbean
*Peter Standish, Series Editor*

GREENWOOD PRESS
Westport, Connecticut • London

**Library of Congress Cataloging-in-Publication Data**

Ferreira, César.
    Culture and customs of Peru / César Ferreira and Eduardo Dargent-Chamot.
       p.   cm.—(Culture and customs of Latin America and the Caribbean, ISSN 1521–8856)
    Includes bibliographical references and index.
    ISBN 0–313–30318–5 (alk. paper)
    1. Peru—Civilization—20th century.   2. Peru—Social life and customs.   3. Arts,
Peruvian—20th century.   I. Dargent-Chamot, Eduardo.   II. Title.   III. Series.
    F3448.F37   2003
    985.06—dc21        2002017114

British Library Cataloguing in Publication Data is available.

Library of Congress Catalog Card Number: 2002017114
ISBN: 0–313–30318–5
ISSN: 1521–8856

First published in 2003

Greenwood Press, 88 Post Road West, Westport, CT 06881
An imprint of Greenwood Publishing Group, Inc.
www.greenwood.com

Printed in the United States of America

The paper used in this book complies with the
Permanent Paper Standard issued by the National
Information Standards Organization (Z39.48–1984).

10  9  8  7  6  5  4  3  2  1

For Dick Gerdes and in memory of Aída Alva-Gerdes.

# Contents

| | |
|---|---|
| Illustrations | ix |
| Series Foreword | xi |
| Acknowledgments | xiii |
| Chronology | xv |
| **1 Context** | **1** |
| **2 Religion and Religious Celebrations** | **37** |
| **3 Social Customs** | **49** |
| **4 Broadcasting and Print Media** | **61** |
| **5 Literature** | **77** |
| **6 Performing Arts and Cinema** | **105** |
| **7 Art, Architecture, and Photography** | **131** |
| Glossary | 153 |
| Selected Bibliography | 157 |
| Index | 161 |

# Illustrations

| | |
|---|---|
| Map of Peru | 2 |
| The Amazon River | 3 |
| District of Miraflores | 5 |
| Girl from Huaraz | 6 |
| Llamas feeding | 10 |
| President Alejandro Toledo (2001) | 31 |
| San Francisco Church, Lima | 38 |
| Procession of the Señor de los Milagros | 43 |
| Women in the Peruvian highlands | 51 |
| Woman with llama, Cuzco | 52 |
| Varieties of dried corn | 57 |
| Inca Garcilaso de la Vega | 81 |
| Novelist Mario Vargas Llosa | 94 |
| Andean musician, Huánuco | 123 |
| "Paisaje Serrano," by Enrique Camino Brent | 135 |
| Machu Picchu | 137 |

City Hall, Lima                                                                  138

District of Miraflores                                                           139

Pedro Campos and José Aguirre, shoe shiners in Lima                              148

Sara Orellana Rodríguez sells religious objects in Lima                          149

Aída Miraval Espinoza sells newspapers in Lima                                   150

# Series Foreword

"CULTURE" is a problematic word. In everyday language we tend to use it in at least two senses. On the one hand we speak of cultured people and places full of culture, uses that imply a knowledge or presence of certain forms of behavior or of artistic expression that are socially prestigious. In this sense large cities and prosperous people tend to be seen as the most cultured. On the other hand, there is an interpretation of "culture" that is broader and more anthropological; culture in this broader sense refers to whatever traditions, beliefs, customs, and creative activities characterize a given community—in short, it refers to what makes that community different from others. In this second sense, everyone has culture; indeed, it is impossible to be without culture.

The problems associated with the idea of culture have been exacerbated in recent years by two trends: less respectful use of language and a greater blurring of cultural differences. Nowadays, "culture" often means little more than behavior, attitude, or atmosphere. We hear about the culture of the boardroom, of the football team, of the marketplace; there are books with titles like *The Culture of War* by Richard Gabriel (Greenwood, 1990) or *The Culture of Narcissism* by Christopher Lasch (1979). In fact, as Christopher Clausen points out in an article published in the *American Scholar* (Summer 1996), we have gotten ourselves into trouble by using the term so sloppily.

People who study culture generally assume that culture (in the anthropological sense) is learned, not genetically determined. Another general assumption made in these days of multiculturalism has been that cultural differences should be respected rather than put under pressure to change.

But these assumptions, too, have sometimes proved to be problematic. For instance, multiculturalism is a fine ideal, but in practice it is not always easy to reconcile with the beliefs of the very people who advocate it: for example, is female circumcision an issue of human rights or just a different cultural practice?

The blurring of cultural differences is a process that began with the steamship, increased with radio, and is now racing ahead with the Internet. We are becoming globally homogenized. Since the English-speaking world (and the United States in particular) is the dominant force behind this process of homogenization, it behooves us to make efforts to understand the sensibilities of members of other cultures.

This series of books, a contribution toward that greater understanding, deals with the neighbors of the United States, with people who have just as much right to call themselves Americans. What are the historical, institutional, religious, and artistic features that make up the modern culture of such peoples as the Haitians, the Chileans, the Jamaicans, and the Guatemalans? How are their habits and assumptions different from our own? What can we learn from them? As we familiarize ourselves with the ways of other countries, we come to see our own from a new perspective.

Each volume in the series focuses on a single country. With slight variations to accommodate national differences, each begins by outlining the historical, political, ethnic, geographical, and linguistic context, as well as the religious and social customs, and then proceeds to a discussion of a variety of artistic activities, including the press, the media, the cinema, music, literature, and the visual and performing arts. The authors are all intimately acquainted with the countries concerned: some were born or brought up in them, and each has a professional commitment to enhancing the understanding of the culture in question.

We are inclined to suppose that our ways of thinking and behaving are normal. And so they are . . . for us. We all need to realize that ours is only one culture among many, and that it is hard to establish by any rational criteria that ours as a whole is any better (or worse) than any other. As individual members of our immediate community, we know that we must learn to respect our differences from one another. Respect for differences between cultures is no less vital. This is particularly true of the United States, a nation of immigrants, but one that sometimes seems to be bent on destroying variety at home, and, worse still, on having others follow suit. By learning about other people's cultures, we come to understand and respect them; we earn their respect for us, and, not least, we see ourselves in a new light.

Peter Standish
East Carolina University

# Acknowledgments

THE AUTHORS wish to thank our colleagues Peter Standish, Richard Pressman, Grady Wray, Luis Cortest, Charles Kenney, and Marcia Haag for their many suggestions while writing this book. Our gratitude also to Dana Loy, Gerardo Castillo, and Andy Peterson for their generous help during the various stages of the manuscript. Finally, a special word of thanks to Wendi Schnaufer and Megan Peckman at Greenwood Press and Nicole Cournoyer at Westchester Book Services for their assistance in the production of the book.

# Chronology

| | |
|---|---|
| 12000–13000 B.C. | Man from Pacaicasa; first human remains on Peruvian soil are discovered. |
| 8000 B.C. | Domestication of hot pepper (*Capsicum chinensis*) (*ají*) and beans (*Phaseolus vulgaris*). |
| 7000 B.C. | Domestication of lima bean (*pallar*). |
| 4000–6000 B.C. | Domestication of corn (*Sea mais*). |
| 4000–3500 B.C. | Domestication of cameloids (guanacos, llamas, and alpacas). |
| 3500–2500 B.C. | Domestication of guinea pig (*Cavia porcelus*). |
| 3000 B.C. | Caral, a pyramidal complex north of Lima, is built. Caral is considered the oldest city in the Americas. |
| 2500 B.C. | First textiles are found. |
| 1800 B.C. | Pottery appears in Huánuco in central Andes. |
| 800 B.C.–A.D. 200 | Development of Chavín culture, the first pan-Andean culture. |
| A.D. 200–400 | Nasca culture flourishes on southern coast of Peru. |
| 200–500 | Moche culture flourishes on northern coast of Peru (Lord of Sipán). |

| | |
|---|---|
| 550–900 | Tiahuanaco and Huari cultures flourish in southern Andes. |
| 1100–1450 | Chimú culture expands in northwestern Peru and the city of Chan-Chan is built. |
| 1200–1400 | Foundation of city of Cuzco by Manco Capac, first of fourteen Incas; formative period of Incas. |
| 1438 | Pachacútec starts Inca expansion; Machu Picchu is built. |
| 1526 | Death of Huayna Cápac ignites civil war among Incas. |
| 1528 | Spanish explorer Francisco Pizarro first arrives in Tumbes. |
| 1532 | Foundation of first Spanish city by the conquistadors, San Miguel de Piura, in northern Peru; Pizarro captures Atahualpa, fourteenth Inca, in Cajamarca in northern Peru. |
| 1533 | Atahualpa is executed. Spaniards capture Cuzco. |
| 1535 | Foundation of city of Lima by Pizarro. |
| 1541 | Pizarro is murdered. |
| 1542 | A high court (Audiencia) is established in Lima, and Spanish crown decrees New Laws to limit enslavement of Indians; Francisco Orellana discovers Amazon River. |
| 1543 | Viceroyalty of Peru is created with Lima as its capital. Blasco Núñez de Vela is named first Viceroy of Peru. |
| 1544–1548 | Civil wars take place between Pizarro's brothers against the Spanish crown. Núñez de Vela dies in coup. |
| 1545 | Discovery of silver mines of Potosí in present-day Bolivia. |
| 1551 | University of San Marcos is founded in Lima. |
| 1568 | First coins are minted in South America in Lima. |
| 1569 | Reorganization of administrative powers under the Viceroyalty of Francisco de Toledo. Political power is |

|      | centralized in Lima and Spanish colonial rule is strengthened. |
|------|---|
| 1570 | Inquisition is established in Lima. |
| 1584 | Arrival of first printing press in Lima. |
| 1609 | El Inca Garcilaso de la Vega, considered first Peruvian writer, publishes *Comentarios Reales*. |
| 1610 | Population of Lima is estimated at 25,000. |
| 1617 | Isabel Flores de Oliva, the first female saint in the Americas, dies in Lima; she is later canonized as Santa Rosa de Lima. |
| 1700 | Bourbons succeed Hapsburgs in the throne of Spain. Philip V, Bourbon grandson of Louis XIV of France, is crowned new king of Spain. |
| 1730 | Bourbonic Reforms are introduced in Europe and the Americas. |
| 1767 | Jesuits are expelled from all territories belonging to Spain and their holdings are confiscated by Spanish crown. |
| 1780–1782 | Rebellion against Spanish crown led by Túpac Amaru II takes place near Cuzco, claiming 100,000 lives. |
| 1789 | The French Revolution takes place, becoming the main ideological source for future independent movements in the Americas. |
| 1790–1795 | Newspaper *Mercurio Peruano* is published, introducing new liberal ideas in Peru. |
| 1808 | Napoleon invades Spain; royal government of Spain collapses. |
| 1820 | After declaring the independence of Argentina and Chile from Spanish rule, General José de San Martín's army arrives in Pisco, south of Lima. The Argentine general leads the first army to liberate Peru from Spanish rule. |
| July 28, 1821 | Declaration of independence in Lima by General San Martín. |

| | |
|---|---|
| 1821–1845 | First years of Peru's republic are marked by great political instability; twenty-four regime changes take place, and constitution is rewritten six times. |
| 1822 | Generals San Martín and Simón Bolívar meet in port of Guayaquil in present-day Ecuador. Bolívar, responsible for the independence of present-day Venezuela, Colombia, and Ecuador, continues struggle in Peru against Spanish crown. |
| 1824 | General Antonio José de Sucre leads patriot army against royalist army in Battle of Ayacucho, sealing Peru's independence. |
| 1829 | War between Peru and Colombia. |
| 1836–1839 | Peru and Bolivia form a confederation. |
| 1854 | Emancipation of slaves by Peruvian president Ramón Castilla. |
| 1863–1875 | Guano (natural fertilizer made from bird manure) boom helps rebuild Peruvian economy. |
| 1866 | War between Peru and Spain; Spanish fleet attacks port of Callao near Lima, but is repulsed and defeated after a brief war. |
| 1871 | Henry Meiggs builds first railroad in southern Peru. |
| 1872 | José Pardo is elected as Peru's first civilian president. |
| 1879–1883 | War between Peru and Chile, known as the War of the Pacific; Peru loses its southern provinces of Tarapacá and Arica to Chile. |
| 1895 | President Nicolás de Piérola modernizes Peruvian state. |
| 1899–1919 | Period of political peace and export-led prosperity known as "Aristocratic Republic." |
| 1919–1930 | President Augusto B. Leguía governs under heavy foreign investment and curtailment of civil liberties. |
| 1924 | Foundation of Alianza Popular Revolucionaria Americana (APRA), one of Peru's oldest political organi- |

zations, by Victor Raúl Haya de la Torre. Its members are popularly known as *apristas*.

| | |
|---|---|
| 1930 | Death of José Carlos Mariátegui, founder of Peruvian Communist Party. |
| 1933–1934 | War between Peru and Colombia over a border dispute. |
| 1941 | War between Peru and Ecuador over a border dispute. |
| 1948 | Coup of General Manuel A. Odría. |
| 1956 | Manuel Prado becomes president in general elections marking the return of democratic rule. Women vote for the first time in a presidential election. |
| 1963 | Fernando Belaúnde is elected president, and democratic rule is restored; Mario Vargas Llosa, Peru's most renowned novelist, publishes *La ciudad y los perros* (The Time of the Hero). |
| 1965 | Guerrilla movements appear in southern Peru. |
| 1968–1980 | Leftist military government of Generals Juan Velasco Alvarado and Francisco Morales Bermúdez inaugurates unprecedented period of economic and social reforms. |
| 1979 | Haya de la Torre, founder of APRA, dies. |
| 1980 | Second government of President Fernando Belaúnde; Shining Path, or Sendero Luminoso, a communist guerrilla movement, launches a guerrilla war against Peruvian state in southern Andes, eventually reaching coastal cities. |
| 1985 | Alan García, the first Aprista president of Peru, is elected. His government is characterized by hyperinflation and social violence. |
| 1990 | Alberto Fujimori is elected president of Peru. |
| 1992 | Abimael Guzmán, leader of Shining Path, is captured. |
| 1992 | Fujimori closes down the Peruvian congress. New congressional elections are held in which he obtains a majority. |

1995      After changing the constitution, Fujimori is reelected president of Peru for a second term.

2000      In fraudulent elections, Fujimori is reelected president of Peru, but amid social unrest and charges of corruption is forced into exile. Valentín Paniagua, president of the Peruvian congress, heads a government of transition.

2001      Alejandro Toledo is elected president of Peru, defeating former President García, who runs for the second time for the presidency as a candidate for APRA.

# 1

# Context

## LAND AND PEOPLE

THE REPUBLIC of Peru is located on the western coast of South America with a surface of 496,225 square miles, an area about three times the size of California. Three very distinct geographical regions—the coastal region or *costa*, the Andes or *sierra*, and the jungle or *selva*—make for three culturally diverse worlds. Peru is divided into twenty-four departments and one constitutional province (the port of Callao, adjacent to Lima). Its geography presents a longitudinal division dominated by the Andes ridge, with its tallest mountains being between 5,000 and 6,000 meters high (some fifteen to 22,000 feet). To the west, a desertic coast crossed by numerous rivers is washed by the Pacific Ocean, rich in fish and other resources.

The rugged geological formation of the Peruvian Andes is formed by three chains that meet in the northern, central, and southern parts of the country, the last knot being a large plateau, also known as the altiplano, where Lake Titicaca is located. Shared with neighboring Bolivia, Lake Titicaca is the highest navigable lake in the world and one of the country's main tourist attractions. The Andean valleys between the eastern, central, and western ranges are fertile and populated, and they house the most productive silver, copper, and gold mines in the country. They are, in fact, where the most important pre-Hispanic developments took place. Cuzco, the capital of the Inca empire, and Cajamarca, where the last Inca was captured by the Spanish conquistador Francisco Pizarro during the sixteenth century, are both in this region of the country.

Map of Peru.

The Amazon River. Photos by Gloria Satizabal de Araneta.

From the eastern slopes of the Andes all the way to the borders of Ecuador, Colombia, Brazil, and Bolivia, the Amazon River basin, crossed by many meandering rivers, stretches like a green carpet and is one of the richest areas of biodiversity in the world. This area was most vital during the rubber boom that lasted from the late nineteenth to the early twentieth century. Once an oil-producing area, it is now rapidly developing into a promising gas-producing region. At the same time, the higher sections are becoming home to the production of the coca leaf, the raw material out of which cocaine is made. If coca crops are a big international and national problem for their moral and legal implications, oil and gas also represent a great danger to Peru's ecosystem if not properly handled. Another product, timber, and the unorganized way in which it is exploited, is also a threat to the area's ecology.

Lima, Peru's capital, is home for one-third of the some 25 million inhabitants of Peru, who in recent decades have migrated from rural areas in the *sierra* and *selva* in search of better living conditions. As a result, Lima is a melting pot of sorts for the country, where the nation's many cultures converge. Other important cities in Peru are Arequipa (634,000 inhabitants), Trujillo (532,000), Cuzco (275,000), Huancayo (200,000), and Iquitos (269,000).

## THE SEA

A cold water current that moves from Antarctica to the equator imposes its influence all along the Peruvian coast. Discovered by the German explorer Alexander von Humbolt in the early nineteenth century, the Humboldt current nurses a large amount of phytoplankton, which is the first link in a food chain responsible for one the most important single export products in Peruvian republican history: guano. Last century, guano, or bird manure, produced over centuries by the millions of sea fowl that live off the region's fish, was exported in large quantities to Europe. This nitrate-rich product infuses tired soils with new life. The pre-Columbian people of Peru used guano to aid their crops, but the technology was lost during the Spanish colonial period. It was not until Humboldt rediscovered its nutritional value that it once again became a useful product.

During the 1950s, the requirements for a low-cost concentrated food product that could satisfy Peru's rapidly developing chicken farms were found in fish meal, made from desiccated and processed anchovies. In fact, since the 1960s, fish meal has been one the richest export products of Peru, although the industry has gone through difficult times due to both overfishing and nationalization of the industry during the leftist General Juan Velasco Alvarado military regime in the 1970s, which brought the industry's boom

District of Miraflores. Photo by Gloria Satizabal de Araneta.

to collapse. At the present time, however, it remains an important industry, a good source of income for the nation.

## THE COAST

Closely related to the sea, the desertic coast is crossed by a series of rivers, and since very early times the region has been developed into fertile valleys by its inhabitants. The construction of canals has allowed the extension of these beneficial waters into large areas won from the sands. The coastal economy has since been associated with agriculture as well as with the sea, the valleys forming a sequence of isolated economic poles breached since antiquity by intervalley navigation and connecting roads. Today, the Pan-American Highway links the Peruvian coast all the way from northern Huaquillas on the Ecuadorian border to the Concordia crossing on the border with Chile. Each valley has its own characteristics and its own products. The northern coastal valleys are known for their rice and sugarcane production, the central valleys are rich in cotton, and their southern counterparts are grape producers. From the coast large amounts of fruits are harvested. Nowadays, large investments into irrigation and other modern technology are being made, allowing the deserts to flourish.

Another important product on the coast is oil from the fields in the de-

Girl from Huaraz. Photo by Gloria Satizabal de Araneta.

partments of Tumbes and Piura in the north. Oil was discovered there during the mid-nineteenth century, and production began in the early twentieth century. In fact, Peruvian oil wells were the first to be exploited in South America. During the early years of General Velasco's military regime (1968–1980), the petroleum industry, then in the hands of Standard Oil Company of New Jersey, was nationalized. However, inefficient government administration plundered oil production, converting Peru, once a self-sufficient oil-producing country with an export surplus, into an importer with heavy dependency on international markets. After the twelve-year military regime, international companies were welcomed again and the country continues to better its position in the world market.

## THE HIGHLANDS

From low-sloping mountains in the north to the Andean trapeze in the south, the Andes cross the country longitudinally. At about the center, the Callejón de Huaylas ridge in the department of Ancash, with the snow-capped Huascarán mountain rising up 6,768 meters (some 18,000 feet above sea level), marks the highest point of the Peruvian Andes. The Callejón de Huaylas ridge, with its many high mountains, is a tourist paradise, both for its scenic beauty and its mountain climbing possibilities.

Located in the southern Andes are the departments of Cuzco and Puno, two of the country's best-known cities. Cuzco is the old Inca capital, where colonial structures are superimposed on ancient imperial buildings. It is located in a picturesque mid-altitude valley. The city of Puno is located nearby on the shores of Lake Titicaca at 3,815 meters above sea level (some 15,000 feet).

## THE JUNGLE

The eastern slopes of the Andes roll down to the Amazon basin, a tropical forest with one of the highest rates of biodiversity on the planet. Large meandering rivers and a green carpet are its most prominent characteristics. The Peruvian jungle is very scarcely populated by a number of diverse native communities, each with its own language and culture, as well as by an increasing group of multiethnic migrants who have been settling there for over a century. Most cities and towns are established on the banks of the biggest rivers, the port of Iquitos on the shores of the Amazon River being the most important, along with the city of Pucallpa over the Ucayali River and the city of Puerto Maldonado on the Madre de Dios River.

## DEMOGRAPHICS AND A PROFILE OF THE PEOPLE OF PERU

With some 25 million inhabitants, Peru's annual growth rate is 1.7%, with an infant mortality rate of forty-three for every 1,000 children. Life expectancy for males is 67 years and for females is 71. Elementary and secondary school enrollment is about 6.1 million, while the country's illiteracy rate is 25.3% in rural areas and an estimated 5.3% in urban areas. Between public and private institutions, Peru has sixty-five universities and an annual enrollment of under 40,000 students.

Peru's economy has a Gross Domestic Product (GDP) of an estimated $54 billion, with an annual growth rate of 3%. Per capita GDP is $2,150. Some 7.6 million Peruvians are part of the work force. The country's exports are mainly copper, fish meal, textiles, zinc, gold, coffee, and sugar, amounting to some $6.8 billion, with the United States being its most important trade partner.

Most Peruvians define themselves as *mestizos,* that is, a people of mixed ethnic origin. This fact reflects a long history of migrations, demographic trends, and a complex social blending process throughout Peruvian history, dating back to the arrival of the Spanish conquistadors in the sixteenth century. Current research estimates that the population of the Inca empire in 1530 was that of some 16 million Indians. However, since the Spanish conquest began in 1532, the population dropped dramatically to under 1 million a century later; such extermination was the result of the social dislocation suffered by the indigenous groups, forced labor, and the arrival of new diseases, such as smallpox and syphilis.

Quechua, the language of the Inca empire, prevailed throughout the Andean region after the conquest was completed and was used by priests that arrived from Spain to convert the Indians to Catholicism. New indigenous communities were created by the Spanish crown to reorganize the natives, following the models of rural Spain, which to a large extent were that of a feudal system. Despite all these changes, the native people of Peru managed to maintain their ancestral customs and thus began a process of cultural amalgamation that evolved with time and permeated the entire social, economic, artistic, and religious life of the Peruvian peasantry in the highlands.

Because of an increasing scarcity in the labor force due to Indian mortality, African slaves started arriving in Peru with Spanish conquistadors in growing number to work as servants and in coastal plantations. After slavery was abolished in 1854, Chinese peasants were brought to Peru to work in the guano industry, the construction of railroads, and agriculture. In the early twentieth century, Japanese farmers arrived in Peru looking for jobs in the cotton and sugar plantations, as well as in the small business sector of cities on the coast. In addition, at different times in Peru's republican history, Jews, Italians, Germans, Eastern Europeans, and Arabs also arrived on its soil, contributing to the ethnic diversity of contemporary Peruvian society. Finally, since the 1940s, massive migrations from the rural areas to the cities on the coast, in search of better jobs and better living conditions, continued changing the social composition of Peru. In fact, the country's urban population has jumped from 35% to 70% in the last three decades. Lima has grown from a city of half a million inhabitants in 1940 to over 7 million in the late 1990s. As a result, because of an ongoing blending process among the population and because the notion of *mestizaje* works as a national ideal, it is misleading to establish sharp ethnic distinctions within the Peruvian population. Nonetheless, it is estimated that in contemporary Peru, 45% of the population is indigenous, 37% is mestizo (a mixture of indigenous and white), 15% is white, and 3% is of African, Japanese, Chinese, or other descent.

While migrants on the coast of Peru and its descendants mostly adopted Spanish as their language, the indigenous peoples of the highlands and the Amazon basin maintained their own mother languages. As of 1993 (the year when the latest data from a national census is available), it was estimated that 80% (15,405,024) of the population that is five years old or older speaks Spanish as its first language; 16% (3,177,938) speaks Quechua; and 2% (440,380) speaks Aymara, another important indigenous tongue spoken in the altiplano. In addition, the Peruvian Amazon is one of the regions with the highest concentration of native languages in the world. Despite the relatively small number of native people who live there (132,172), sixty-five different ethno-linguistic groups exist, including the Ashaninka, the Aguaruna, the Machiguenga, and the Shipibo-Conibo. While, as a whole, this ethnic diversity has produced a culturally rich and diverse society, it has also resulted in an economically and racially divided social structure, with a large gap between rich and poor. In fact, 54% of the population lives under the poverty line, with 70% of poor Peruvians concentrated in rural areas. As is the case of many countries throughout Latin America, Peru's remaining challenge as a society in years ahead is the consolidation of all its citizens into one strong nation.

## HISTORY

The earliest civilization found in Peru is Chavín, and its cultural center is located on the central Andean Callejón de Huaylas region near a village that gives it its name: Chavín de Huantar. The culture of Chavín developed around 1000 B.C. and lasted until the year 200 of our era.

Early human groups that inhabited Peruvian territory provided a very bare-bones cultural framework from which later Peruvians could build. The many pre-Columbian cultures that developed from the time of Chavín until the arrival of the Spaniards in 1532 worked hard to better their lives in many areas.

Llamas feeding. Photo by Gloria Satizabal de Araneta.

### Domestication

The central Andes is one of the few places in the world where domestication of plants and animals took place during the Neolithic Age. In the Americas, Peru shares that distinction with Mexico. The most famous plant domesticated in ancient Peru was the potato, a crop that in time saved Europeans from their periodic famine cycles. Corn (maize), although found in ancient Andean cultures, is most likely a Mexican development. There are, however, some experts who argue a probable Andean origin. Many other vegetables, fruits, and grains, now known around the world for their great nutritional value, such as beans, sweet potatoes, quinoa, avocados, hot pepper (*ají*), and peanuts, also originated in Peru.

The llama and the alpaca were among the most important animal species domesticated early on in the Americas. Both of these animals are producers of wool and meat. Larger than the alpaca, the llama has a coarser type of wool, and was used to carry loads. Also important was the vicuña, a relative of the previous two, known for its fine wool, which remains an important source of income for Andean villagers and one of the country's best-known export products. Another animal of importance was the guinea pig, or *cuy*. *Cuy* is still consumed for its tasty meat in the *sierra*, but in ancient times in the Andes it was also an important symbol in various religious practices.

### Water Control

A surprising aspect of ancient Andean culture was the highly developed systems created to control water for agricultural purpose. These irrigation systems allowed for maximum production of fields in a difficult geographical region such as the Andes and enlargement of the agricultural frontier of pre-Columbian Peru. Some of these include the following:

#### Canals

From the time of early pre-Columbian cultures there developed a vast network of artificial waterways all over the country. The oldest canalization known is the Cumbemayo channel near Cajamarca. The Cumbemayo canal has been associated with the Chavín influence and, therefore, has been in use since the beginning of the modern era. In the valley of Cañete south of Lima, the Socci canal was already in use when the Incas conquered the coast in the mid-fifteenth century. Today, it remains an important source of irrigation for a large part of the valley.

#### Andenes

These terracelike structures not only allow for efficient irrigation but also have underground areas made of leaves that work like sponges to store residual waters for dry periods. They can be found all along the Peruvian Andes. Outside the city of Cuzco, especially on the trip to Machu Picchu, *andenes* are a common sight.

#### Camellones

In the areas near Lake Titicaca, the pre-Columbian peoples built mud structures about a foot over the level of the soil so that when the lake rose, there was dry land to plant. The level of the lake remains low during the wet season, but due to the flatness of the grounds of the altiplano, the water covers a large area, keeping the sides of the plantations wet. A visitor to the area can see this system of agriculture still in use.

#### Islas flotantes

Built with several layers of *totora* reeds (tall reeds originally found along the northern coast but later transplanted along the coast of Lake Titicaca) and covered with soil, the floating islands of Lake Titicaca (Taquile and Uros) are a unique feature. The Uros people were a human group that in antiquity occupied a large area of southern Peru and finally retreated to the interior of the lake for protection, where they remain today, occupying the *islas flotantes.*

### The Use of the Sea

Early humans on the coast of Peru collected shells and other seafood from the sand and rocks. Sea mammals, especially sea lions, were also captured. Hooks, first made from shells and thorns, and later of metal, allowed early fishermen to enlarge the number of sea products they could consume. They made nets with stones tied to the bottom and gourds as floaters at the top. Physical anthropologists studying early coastal men's ears have found enlargements produced by constant diving for crabs, shellfish, and similar animals. When their job required fishermen to leave the collection of shore prey to go into the open sea, different vessels were developed. Of these, the best known is the *caballito de totora*, a name given by the Spaniards to boats made from *totora* reed. People ride the boats in a position similar to sitting on a horse, with both legs in the water. The efficiency of these boats is demonstrated by their continued use to this day on the northern coast. The areas of Trujillo and Chiclayo are good places to see them in action. The *caballitos de totora* of Lake Titicaca were introduced in the altiplano during the Inca empire by coastal artisans sent there especially for that purpose.

## THE INCA EMPIRE

Of all the peoples of ancient Peru, it is the Incas of whom we know the most—not only because of available archaeological remains, but because early Spanish chroniclers left a large quantity of information regarding their social, economic, political, and cultural life. Also, since the Inca descendents have survived along with their language (Quechua), religion, and mores, it is possible to know more about their lifestyle.

Although scientific evidence makes clear that the Quechua civilization from Cuzco developed into a state sometime during A.D. 1100 or 1200, the mythological beginnings recorded by Spanish chroniclers speak of a divine couple, Manco Cápac and his sister-wife Mama Ocllo, both children of the Sun God, who emerged from Lake Titicaca. Their father had given them a golden baton, instructing them that wherever it could penetrate totally into the soil, they should begin an empire. The soil proved soft enough in the valley of Cuzco, in the southern Andes, where they established their kingdom.

Another legend speaks of four brothers who came out of the Tamputoco mountain led by Ayar Manco. The group also included Ayar Manco's brothers, Ayar Uchu, Ayar Auca, and Ayar Cachi, along with their respective wives. From nearby areas, other groups also became followers of the Ayar brothers. During their journey, Uchu, Auca, and Cachi died. Shortly after, Ayar Manco and his accompanying group arrived in the valley, and they went to the place where the mythical golden bar had gone deeply into fertile ground. Manco and his followers founded the city of Cuzco after subduing some native peoples who lived in the area.

The history of the Incas is divided between the Urin, or Lower empire, and the Hanan, or Higher empire. Over a period of 300 years, fourteen Incas ruled over an expanding territory known as the Tahuantinsuyo.

The social system of the Incas had an ancient Andean origin based on the *ayllu*, an extended family group with a common ancestor. The economic system was also based on ancient social structures and can be explained through several principles, namely reciprocity, redistribution, and vertical control. Reciprocity was of two kinds: symmetrical reciprocity, which were projects among equals who called to help each other with tasks, such as building a house; and asymmetrical reciprocity, which could be in the form of communal work to support the religious and political structures of the empire, such as working on the lands of lords, or road or canal building and maintenance. Redistribution, a practice employed by the state, ensured that all agricultural goods not exchanged by reciprocity were to be distributed in different areas of the empire in case of bad crops. Part of that surplus was used to support the army and, in special cases, as gifts for nobles. Finally, vertical control was a form of political and social organization that allowed economic self-sufficiency for any community. In fact, vertical control assured a way by which communities or *ayllus* could receive a variety of products needed (from fish of the coast to cattle products found in the highest terrains of the Andes), by placing members of those *ayllus* at different ecological levels throughout the empire. For example, *ayllus* occupied lands in the high mountains dedicated to llamas and alpacas, and other lands in mid-altitude to harvest corn or other products. Some *ayllus* even had lands on the coast to look over fish and guano production, as well as in the entry area of the tropical Amazonic forest in order to collect honey, colorful feathers, fruits, and wood.

The most powerful ruler of the empire was the Inca. A patriarchal figure, he was believed to be the son of the Sun God and, therefore, divine himself. He ruled all aspects of life in the empire. Through him the harmony of the universe was kept. As symbols of servility, his subjects could not look him straight in the eye and had to bear heavy burdens on their backs when in his presence.

The Inca was the head of his family group, or *panaka*. Each Inca started his own *panaka*. Upon the Inca's death, his descendents were given the obligation of caring for their founder's mummified body. Some Spanish chroniclers claim that these family groups apparently functioned as a sort of political elite or interest group. As a new Inca reached power, the governing elite multiplied, creating a larger and larger aristocracy in the empire, as well as new political struggles. The expansion of this elite eventually brought about strong political disputes that would create a political crisis between the last two Incas, Huáscar and Atahualpa, which also coincided with the arrival of the Spanish conquistadors.

The main wife of the Inca was the *Coya*. Sometimes, she was also the ruler's sister. In fact, polygamy was often practiced by the ruling Inca as a way of strengthening his political influence. Therefore, the Inca had other wives, many of whom were related to local chieftains of other ethnic groups in the empire, whom he married in order to expand and secure new political alliances. All these women and their children became part of the royal *panaka*. Below the Inca and his immediate family was the Inca nobility headed by the *Orejones*, or men of big ears, who received their name from the practice beginning in childhood of enlarging their ears by means of round wooden ornaments introduced in a hole made in the ear lobe. Only individuals of the highest nobility could become *Orejones*. It was believed these nobles belonged to the families who had accompanied the Ayar brothers on their original journey to Cuzco. Immediately below them were those members of families that joined the original group in their march to Cuzco, followed by the provincial nobility and chieftains who had been made members of the ruling class by the Inca in recognition of special service.

The priesthood was headed by the Inca's brother, or *Willac Umo*; all others in charge of the religious administration of the empire were appointed by the Inca himself, especially when dealing with the official worship of the Sun God, Wiracocha. The conquered peoples within the empire were allowed to keep their own gods and, therefore, had their own religious structures. The commoners of the empire, called Hatun Runa, were mostly farmers. They were divided by provinces, sex, and age. Each male received a piece of land called a *tupu*, while women received half that same extension of land.

The *Mitamicunas*, or Mitmac, were sections of the population transferred to other parts of the empire as colonizers, usually to control the natives of the area on behalf of the Inca state in the recently conquered lands. It has been suggested that the *Mitamicunas* were groups that had been punished and barred from their original land. One of the interesting facts about the *Mitamicunas* is that they were always transferred to places with climate, altitude, and living conditions similar to their own, suggesting careful governmental planning.

The *Yanacunas*, or Yanas, were a social group in charge of menial tasks. Some historians argue that they were slaves who had been punished.

## The Inca Roads

The Inca empire was divided into four regions: Chinchaysuyo, Antisuyo, Collasuyo, and Contisuyo. One of its most interesting features was the road system that crossed its territory in every direction, uniting the empire. Two main longitudinal roads moved from south to north, one along the coast and one through the mountains. A series of transversal routes connected those roads through the valleys. It has been estimated that the Cápac Ñam, as this communication system was called, covered some 10,000 miles.

Bridges allowed road users—mainly the Inca messengers, or runners, known as *chasquis*—to cross rivers and in a short time travel between places as distant as Quito and Cuzco. The Spanish chroniclers were surprised to learn that due to the *chasqui* system, the Incas could eat fresh seafood in Cuzco. There was a rest station about every twelve miles, a distance runners could cover in about one hour. At each rest station, they passed on the message or product they were carrying to another *chasqui* so that they could be delivered around the clock.

## The End of the Inca Empire

According to the traditional version left by Spanish chroniclers, the Inca empire fell as a result of a power struggle between two pretenders to the throne: Huáscar and Atahualpa. Before his death in 1526, their father, Huayna Cápac, had supposedly divided the empire between his two sons. Cuzco was to be ruled by Huáscar and Quito by Atahualpa. While Huáscar, the oldest son, was Huayna Cápac's legitimate child, Atahualpa was considered an illegitimate offspring. The son of a Quitenian princess, Atahualpa plotted a takeover of the entire empire according to the chroniclers. However, this version of events is strictly based on European principles of inheritance, where the oldest son directly took over the throne of any given kingdom. However, according to more current scholars of Peruvian history, Huayna Cápac never divided the empire. These historians further dismiss a European idea of inheritance to a throne since such a notion had no correlation in the Andean world. Nevertheless, it is worth remembering that the Spanish conquistadors accused Atahualpa of fratricide and usurpation of power in order to execute him in 1533 and continue their bloody conquest of the empire.

According to traditional historians, Francisco Pizarro and his men were able to control the territory and its people by virtue of three factors. The first was their cultural superiority, as demonstrated by their religion, horses, and arms. A second factor, according to the traditional view, was the help they received from God. Along with the help of the Virgin Mary, the Spanish conquistadors believed in the aid of Santiago Matamoros (St. James the Moor killer), who in the Americas became known as St. James the Indian killer. A third factor was the help received from the local population, which was tired of Inca oppression. However, thanks to ethnohistory studies, there has been a critical revision of the end of the Inca empire.

### An Updated View

According to recent research, there are four main elements to be taken into consideration in dealing with the end of the Inca empire: the religious, the political, the economic, and the social.

#### Religious Aspects

A crisis was produced by the founding of Tumibamba, a town near Quito and far from Cuzco. In order to expand and organize the administration of the northern territories, Huayna Cápac stayed there an exceedingly long time. Tumibamba became a place of great religious prestige; it was not only a replica of Cuzco but also an Inca residence. Now a parallel and competing axis of the world had been created, rivaling Cuzco. Its creation meant a rupture in the Incas' unitary structure. Suddenly, Cuzco found its religious, political, and economic privileges weakened. This was enough to cause an upheaval among the Orejones, those in charge of the administration and of the Cuzquenian army.

During this time, the Incas were militarily defeated in Pasto (near Colombia). Such a defeat lowered army morale and brought about a shortage of food in the area, which was soon interpreted as a sign of the wrath of God. Such a crisis was blamed on the long period that the soldiers spent away from the sacred space that was Cuzco. Soon, the *Orejones* decided to remove the Solar Disc (considered a divine icon representing the Sun God) from the Tumibamba temple and return it to Cuzco, thus becoming the token defenders of the Empire's unity. At that time, Huayna Cápac, the twelfth Inca, had to ask for the oracle of Tumibamba back in order to calm his army's discontent; he then proceeded to give his soldiers goods and honors, along with the promise of a prompt return to Cuzco. However, on the way back to Cuzco, Huayna Cápac died of smallpox.

#### Political Aspect

In addition to the religious problem, there was also a political problem due to the confrontation between the Cuzquenian and Quitenian elites. The long stay away from Cuzco by Huayna Cápac created a parallel bureaucracy that weakened the Cuzco group. There is also a suspicion that the succession problem might have been associated to the alternating power of the different *panakas*, but more research is needed on this topic.

### Succession Crisis

After Huayna Cápac's death, the gods were consulted in order to learn if Huáscar should assume the throne. The ritual gave no answer, and a new candidate's name was requested. Soon after, Prince Ninan Coyuchi died of smallpox, just as his father Huayna Cápac had done before him, thus leaving Huáscar and Atahualpa as the only two heirs to the throne. Atahualpa had fought beside his father and had the backing of the powerful chieftains of the Mantaro and Chincha valleys in the central Andes, while Huáscar had stayed in Cuzco, governing the city and pledging to fight only at the last moment when he was made prisoner.

A mythical version of events explains that, during the war, Atahualpa, while in captivity by Huáscar's army, was visited by the prince Amaru Yupanqui, the *auqui*, or aid, of the greatest of all Incas, Pachacútec. Thanks to Amaru Yupanqui, Atahualpa was transformed into a snake by a divinity and escaped through a hole in the ground. This myth tells us of a ritual that unites the three worlds: the earth, the underground, and heaven, since special snakes were also empowered to fly. After his liberation, Atahualpa became unbeatable in the eyes of his people, finally winning the war against his brother Huáscar.

### Economic Aspect

The need to feed and pay a growing army began to put pressure on the Inca redistributive capacity. The conquest of poor lands in northern Ecuador and southern Colombia, as well as the increasing number of bureaucrats, took a toll on the empire's economic system, contributing to its collapse. The northern territory of the empire, the Chinchaysuyo, was the largest of all four regions, but it only had four administrative centers: Cajamarca, Tumibamba, Chachapoyas, and Pumpu. With each passing day, it became more expensive to collect and distribute the goods needed.

### Social Aspect

The non-Cuzquenian elite, and particularly the ethnic lords, were unhappy because the Inca state required more and more from them. They were losing power because they could not control their surplus in products and labor, while the Incas were unable to fulfill their reciprocity obligations.

## FRANCISCO PIZARRO AND THE SPANISH CONQUEST OF PERU

The Spanish conquest of Peru reached its high point with the capture of the last Inca, Atahualpa, in the main plaza of Cajamarca in northern Peru on November 16, 1532. However, it is useful to take a close look at the process that led to this turning point in Peru's history.

In 1513, Francisco Pizarro, a member of conquistador Vasco Núñez de Balboa's army, was already a rich captain and the mayor of the city of Panama, the capital of the present-day republic of Panama. Along with Diego de Almagro, a soldier like himself, and Hernando de Luque, a priest, Pizarro agreed to join forces in an attempt to conquer the Inca empire. Almagro was to help obtain supplies and men, while Luque was in charge of funding. By 1526, after several tentative trips south and no shortage of ordeals, thirteen men reached Tumbes, where the Spaniards confirmed the existence of the Inca empire. Pizarro and his men returned to Panama and soon went on to Spain to negotiate with the Spanish crown the terms of the conquest of Peru. On July 26, 1529, Pizarro signed the Capitulaciones de Toledo, an agreement with the crown by which he received the title of governor of Peru. In addition, Almagro received the title of mayor of the fortress of Tumbes, and Luque the bishopry of Tumbes and the title of "protector of the Indians." The other thirteen men received the title of *hidalgos*, or Spanish knights.

Back in Panama, Pizarro organized an army of 180 men and thirty-seven horses. On January 20, 1531, the expedition left for the conquest of Peru. They reached Tumbes by April, only to find that the city had been destroyed by Inca forces. The expedition continued on to Piura, where they founded the first Spanish city in Peru, San Miguel de Piura, before they decided to challenge the Inca army. After a difficult trip through the Andes, Pizarro's army reached Cajamarca, where Atahualpa was resting with his troops outside the city after defeating his brother Huáscar in civil war.

In Cajamarca, the Spaniards hid near the main plaza while Atahualpa received a group headed by the soldier Hernando de Soto. Atahualpa agreed to meet with the Spaniards the following day, but, in reality, both parties were planning to capture their opponent. The afternoon of November 16, 1532, Atahualpa arrived with his army in Cajamarca's main plaza, carried on a golden litter. Because he saw no one, he thought the Spaniards were afraid. Soon, he was approached by the Dominican friar Vicente Valverde, who was traveling with Pizarro. With the aid of an interpreter, Valverde asked the Inca to convert to Christianity and become a subject of the king of Spain. Valverde handed the Inca the Bible, but Atahualpa threw the book to the ground and angrily told Valverde that the Spaniards must return all they had stolen since their arrival. Shortly after, the Spaniards attacked. Pizarro was the first to reach the Inca, and after the Inca's litter carriers were killed, Atahualpa was made prisoner. In exchange for his freedom, Atahualpa offered Pizarro a roomful of gold and two roomfuls of silver as high as his arm could reach, (Atahualpa's cell, known as the *cuarto del rescate*, can still be visited in Cajamarca) Pizarro accepted Atahualpa's offer and gold and silver objects quickly reached Cajamarca. Before the rooms were filled, Inca troop movements in the surrounding areas and Pizarro's lack of patience forced Pizarro to accept a trial in which Atahualpa was quickly condemned to die by fire. Atahualpa was accused of heresy, of killing his brother Huáscar, and of incest with his sisters, along with other fabricated crimes. To avoid fire, since once burned his mummy could not be preserved to live again according to the Inca tradition, Atahualpa accepted baptism, and was executed at day's end on July 26, 1533.

Later, Pizarro moved toward Cuzco, taking with him as ally one of Atahualpa's brothers, Túpac Hualpa, who had been crowned as a puppet Inca. On the way south, Túpac Hualpa was probably poisoned. Soon after, another prince, Manco Inca, who had survived the civil war, came in contact with the Spaniards. Manco Inca was crowned Inca and marched with the Spaniards into Cuzco after defeating the last troops opposing the invasion. Once there, the Spaniards found no resistance and proceeded to sack the palaces and temples. On March 23, 1524, Pizarro founded the Spanish city of Cuzco, to be built on the ruins of the Inca capital.

### The Founding of Lima

The proximity to the sea, the fertile soil, and the good water quality were the main elements that convinced Pizarro to establish the capital of his government on the coast of the Rimac valley. The founding ceremony took place on January 18, 1535, and the city received the name of City of the Kings of Lima, or Ciudad de los Reyes de Lima. The name refers to the magi, or three wise men, since the soldiers who were sent to choose a place for the city's settlement left on January 6, a day consecrated by the Catholic Church to the wise men of the Orient. Today, the term *Ciudad de los Reyes* is used in a literary form to refer to the kings of Spain, but the coat of arms of the city, given by the Emperor Charles V, shows the three crowns and the star of Bethlehem.

Lima became the economic, political, and cultural center of Spanish colonial life in Peru, while the Andes were a source of wealth because of their many gold and silver mines. Soon, however, the Indian population became victim of the Spaniards' greed. Estimates of population decimation vary, but historians agree that of a population between 12 and 16 million Indians at the time of the Spanish arrival, less than half remained a century later, thanks to disease and the miserable working conditions in the mines.

Civil turmoil developed between the Spaniards when two parties were formed: that of Pizarro, who had received more titles and lands, and that of his partner, Almagro. Almagro felt he had been treated unjustly and considered that Cuzco belonged to the territory he had received from the king of Spain. A civil war ensued, resulting in the eventual assassination of Pizarro in 1541 inside the governmental palace.

### The Viceroyalty of Peru

The viceroyalty of Peru was established in 1543 when the king of Spain named Blasco Núñez de Vela the first viceroy of Peru, the king's direct representative. In Peru's colonial history, there were to be forty such viceroys. Núñez de Vela brought with him the Nuevas Leyes de Indias, a new set of laws announced by the Spanish crown, which in theory protected the Indians from exploitation and restrained conquerors' power. But such laws were seen by the conquistadors as an interference in their domains, so a long period of armed resistance followed. Under Núñez de Vela's rule, a new order was imposed in Peru, with Indians who had been living in the countryside now congregated into new Spanish-style towns to make tax collections and conversions to Christianity easier. Lima became the center of courtly life in a European-like manner, much like Mexico City.

### The Economy of Colonial Peru

Peru's colonial economy was based on the monopoly held by Spain, which mandated that all exports from Spanish territories be sent directly to Europe. In turn, all products purchased by Peruvians had to be brought from Spain. At first, the economy of the new territories was based on the gold looted from temples and graves. However, in 1545 the silver mines of Potosí (in what is modern-day Bolivia) were discovered, increasing the Spanish crown's wealth significantly. Using an Indian name, *mita*, based on the ancient forms of collective cooperation of the *ayllu*, the Spaniards created an institution to force the Indians to work in the mines and pay taxes on their earnings. It was, in fact, a form of slave labor, mandatory for all men.

### The Inquisition

The Inquisition, an institution first created by the Catholic Church to fight heresy (and, by extension, political opposition) in Europe, arrived in

Perú with viceroy Francisco de Toledo in 1570, and lasted during much of the colonial period in Peru until the reformist Cortes de Cádiz abolished it in Spain in 1814. The Inquisition had no power over the Indians, for its domain was only over Spaniards and other people of European origin. In its nearly 250 years in existence in Peru, the Inquisition tried some 3,000 cases, which resulted in 371 persons being sentenced. Of these, only forty were sentenced to death. However, many others were sent to prison or labor camps where they perished. Torture was a common practice used to extract confessions from the accused, and although the percentage of accused who were found guilty and sent to the stake was low, many individuals were crippled for life due to inhuman interrogation procedures. When the Inquisition was abolished, the people of Lima showed their hatred for the institution by assaulting and destroying its offices.

### The End of the Spanish Presence in Peru

By the end of the eighteenth century, the ideas of the Enlightenment had reached Peru through the United States in the French independence of 1776 and French Revolution of 1789. Juan Pablo Viscardo y Guzmán, a priest who left Peru when Jesuits were expelled from all Spanish colonies in 1767, authored the *Carta a los Españoles Americanos* in 1792, a document in which he explained the many differences between Spaniards from Spain and those living in the colonies. In short, it was an expression of a difference in spirit between the people born in Spanish America with respect to the peninsula.

The first important movement toward independence in Peru took place in 1780 when José Gabriel Condorcanqui, a chieftain of Tungasuca, near Cuzco, killed Antonio de Arriaga, the Spanish crown's local representative after denouncing his abuses of the local population. A descendant of the last Inca, Condorcanqui soon took the name Túpac Amaru II and organized an army to rebel against Spanish occupation. After several battles, he was captured and executed in the main plaza of Cuzco in 1781 as four horses pulled on each of his extremities.

## INDEPENDENCE

In the early nineteenth century, while Peruvians prepared for political independence thanks to an organization of liberal thinkers known as Sociedad Amantes del País, led by Hipólito Unanue, the Argentine general, José de San Martín, launched a massive military campaign that resulted in the independence of Argentina and Chile from Spanish rule. By 1820, his army had reached the port of Pisco, south of Lima, and prepared a successful military attack against Lima the following year.

After independence was proclaimed by José de San Martín on July 28, 1821, Peruvians had to choose among three political roads. The establishment of a monarchy was backed by San Martín, largely due to the poor experiences of the newly born republican governments in Argentina and Chile, which he had also liberated. Backing San Martín were conservative sectors of society. A Napoleonic-style government with an authoritarian head of state was favored by Simón Bolívar, the liberator of Venezuela, Colombia, and Ecuador. Finally, a republican form of government, based on the ideals of the American and French revolutions, was backed by liberals and the more progressive sectors of the society. This last option was, in fact, to prevail.

After a historic 1822 meeting with Simón Bolívar in Guayaquil (in what is present-day Ecuador) San Martín abandoned Peru, and the republic was established. It was Bolívar who would complete the Argentine general's ambition for independence. Meanwhile, forces in the newly created congress were divided among liberals, who supported the end of privileges for the *criollos* (Peruvians of European descent), a decentralization of power, and the separation of church and state, and conservatives, who defended a strong central power of divine inspiration, based on the principles of authority and order. In fact, after the final surrendering of Spanish troops in the battle of Ayacucho on December 9, 1824, the only organized institution that could deal with the social, political, and economic problems of the country was the army. Many of the military who had participated in the process of independence took an active role in government. Thus, a nation founded on the principles of reason and the ideals of justice and social equality was soon under the control of military strongmen known as *caudillos*, which would become a long-standing tradition in the history of Latin America.

### President Ramón Castilla

During the second decade of the republic, an idea that had been previously envisioned by Bolívar became a reality: the union of Peru and Bolivia under a confederation. However, due to foreign as well as national interests, the confederation served only to create more social unrest and civil war, eventually leading to the creation of Bolivia as a separate nation. It was not until the governments of Ramón Castilla (1845–1851; 1855–1862) that the country was finally organized and its first budget was presented to congress. Castilla is also famous for abolishing the Indian tribute, an unjust taxation inherited from the Spanish regime that had to be paid by the Indian population. Moreover, it was Castilla who decreed the end of black slavery in Peru in 1854.

### The Guano Boom and the Railroad

Between 1840 and 1860, Peru experienced an important economic boom thanks to the exploitation and exportation of guano (sea bird droppings used as fertilizer). The wealth that the country received helped develop a banking system and other financial institutions that were of great importance for the country's prosperity. This was also the period of railroad construction. The man responsible for most of the new communication systems that crossed Peru from the coast to the cities of the interior was the American builder Henry Meiggs, who began his train experience in Chile building the Valparaíso-Santiago railroad. Later, he was hired by the Peruvian government to build the railroad that linked the southern coastal port of Mollendo with the city of Arequipa, and then with Puno in the altiplano. The engineering task was collosal, but Meiggs achieved his goal in a shorter time than expected, largely due to his organizational genius. Eventually, Meiggs began construction of the railroad from the port of Callao, which serves Lima, to the city of La Oroya in the central Andes. Although Meiggs never saw this project completed, he is still considered the mastermind of the highest railroad in the world.

Because of his engineering and financial innovations, Meiggs is remembered also for the important role he played in the development of democracy in Peru. José Balta, president from 1868 to 1872, was a colonel with modern ideas and a friend of Meiggs and ran for a second term in office in 1872. He was defeated by the first civilian candidate ever to run for the presidency, Manuel Pardo. Meiggs, testifying to his experience of democratic republican rule in the United States, convinced Balta that he should accept the will of the people. Balta well knew how much was at risk for the country's institutional future and accepted his political defeat, marking a turning point in the history of Peru.

### The War with Chile

The good times of guano, and later nitrate wealth, were to come to a sudden end due to a war with Chile in 1879 that had terrible consequences. Peru had signed a military alliance treaty with Bolivia in 1873, and when Chile decided to attack Bolivia in order to capture its nitrate fields in the Antofagasta region, Peru became involved in the conflict, which lasted from 1879 to 1883. During the war, the Peruvian economy collapsed. Many coastal farms were burned, banks were closed, and the city of Lima was occupied by Chilean troops. As a result, the nation's infrastructure was severely damaged. Thousands of lives were lost in the conflict. Despite the courageous actions of some of Peru's greatest heros (Miguel Grau, Francisco Bolognesi, Alfonso Ugarte, and Andrés A. Cáceres), the country suffered severe economic hardship for years. When the war ended, Peru was forced to sign a treatise that permitted the ceding of several southern provinces to Chile. It would take nearly a decade for recovery to begin, with the reforms of a new president.

## The Aristocratic Republic

In 1895, Nicolás de Piérola became president. During his term, arrangements were made to cancel Peru's foreign debt, leaving the country in good standing for future development. Good economic policy led to years of growth in what was later known as the República Aristocrática, a historical period marked by mostly civilian presidents who belonged to the upper class.

In 1919, Augusto Leguía became president after a civilian coup against congress, with the support of the military. Leguía changed the constitution so that he could run for a second consecutive term, and he eventually modified the law so that he could stay in office indefinitely. The Leguía period, known as the eleven-year period, or *el oncenio*, saw the growth of the middle class and the modernization of Peru's institutions. It included instituting the eight-hour workday for the working class.

Leguía's long rule coincided with the triumph of the Bolshevik Revolution in Russia and the consequent rethinking of political ideology in Europe. During this period, two of Peru's most important political thinkers appeared on the national political scene: Victor Raúl Haya de la Torre and José Carlos Mariátegui. In 1924, Haya de la Torre founded the Alianza Popular Revolucionaria Americana (APRA), a political party based on Marxist teachings but nationalistic in nature. Haya de la Torre's political doctrine, known as *aprismo*, which would gain a wide ideological following throughout Latin America, defended national sovereignty and opposed the exploitation of the country's resources by foreign powers. His doctrine also sought the integration of the Indian population into Peru's national reality. Although in time *aprismo* would move rightward as Haya de la Torre aged, it gathered the support of the middle and working classes, making APRA an important participant in Peru's political life during the remainder of the twentieth century.

During that same period, journalist and author José Carlos Mariátegui also became an influential political thinker. He was exiled by Leguía and after four years in Europe, where he immersed himself in the writings of Marx, Engels, and Lenin, Mariátegui became a staunch defender of the Indigenist Movement, which underscored the virtues of Andean culture. Upon his return from Europe, he published his classic work, *Seven Interpretive Essays on Peruvian Reality* (1928), in which he attempted to adapt Marxism to Peruvian reality. Mariátegui then founded the Peruvian Socialist Party, which later became the Peruvian Communist Party. He saw ancient Andean social organization and the participation of *campesinos* as the backbone of a social revolution that would change the social and economic structure of Peru as a nation.

Both Haya de la Torre and Mariátegui changed the nature of Peru's political identity, bringing Peru's middle and working classes into the public debate. In the years to come, APRA would play an important role in Peru's republican history, finally winning control of the government with the presidency of Alan García (1985–1990).

Leguía's third term in office coincided with the Great Depression of 1929. And since the Peruvian economy depended heavily on loans and capital from the United States, the economic shock, along with the corruption surrounding his administration, led to a coup d'état that deposed Leguía in 1930.

With Leguía's fall, a new militarist period began with President Luis Sánchez Cerro, first as head of a junta, and later as an elected president. A strong opponent of APRA, Sánchez Cerro was murdered in 1933, allegedly by a member of this party. He was replaced by another military man, General Oscar R. Benavides, who completed Sánchez Cerro's term, extending his own rule until 1939. Benavides's government had to deal with a border dispute with Colombia. Domestically, he directed his efforts toward limited reform, granting amnesty to political prisoners, among whom was Haya de la Torre, and allowing for the free activity of all political parties. However, once the dispute with Colombia was resolved and the owner of *El Comercio*, Peru's most important daily newspaper, was assassinated by a member of APRA, political persecutions began once again.

A return to democracy was reached when Manuel Prado, a member of one of Peru's wealthiest families, was elected president in 1939 with the backing of the richest sectors of the country, as well as supporters of APRA and the Peruvian Communist Party. During Prado's administration, Peru fought a costly border war with Ecuador between 1941 and 1942. The war ended with a Peruvian victory, but it opened a wound that would not be settled until 1998, after a long period of alternate military skirmishes and negotiations.

Prado's term was followed by a coalition of several political forces, which placed José Luis Bustamante y Rivero in office in 1945. Bustamante y Rivero was a respected democrat and won by a landslide. Unfortunately, political disagreements between his supporters soon led his administration to economic and political instability. And despite the president's efforts to maintain a democratic government, he was overthrown in 1948 in a coup headed by General Manuel A. Odría, who sent Bustamante y Rivero into exile and put Peru, once again, under military rule.

Odría and his military junta governed Peru with an iron fist. During the first two years of his administration, Odría implemented economic measures that stabilized the country's economy. He was aided by an increase in exports of many raw materials and of rice, a product much in demand because of the Korean War. Economic growth soon became apparent in the growth of social spending and a better purchasing power for the population. Odría was a hands-on politician, investing a large part of the country's budget in housing projects, schools, and hospitals, which earned him the backing of all sectors of the population. In 1950, Odría's government called for general elections, with Odría himself aspiring for the presidency. He was challenged by General Ernesto Montagne, whom Odría eventually imprisoned so he could run as an only candidate. He of course won the election and was a constitutionally elected president until 1956, when Manuel Prado was once again elected president. In that election, women were allowed to vote for the first time in Peruvian history.

Prado's second term was stable, making it seem as if the country had reached a more permanent level of democracy. However, shortly before the end of his term in 1962, the military once again stepped in, overthrowing Prado and sending him into exile, while ignoring election results that would have made APRA's Haya de la Torre Peru's next president. A junta was established that would call for new elections in 1963.

That year, Fernando Belaúnde, the leader of Acción Popular, a right-wing party supported by wealthy sectors of society and young Peruvian technocrats, was elected president. An architect by profession, Belaúnde initiated important development projects to strengthen the country's infrastructure and its democracy. One of Belaúnde's main projects was an ambitious plan to build a highway in the Peruvian jungle, eventually linking Colombia, Venezuela, and Bolivia. However, Belaúnde's good intentions soon fell short. His government was marked by a major economic crisis and, in 1965, the rise of a leftist guerrilla group inspired by the Cuban Revolution, which tarnished his administration's image. When effective military action was taken against the rebels, the event reinforced the role of the armed forces in

Peru. Belaúnde's administration had also proved unsuccessful in negotiating a favorable contract for oil exploitation with the U.S.-owned International Petroleum Company in northern Peru.

## The 1968 Coup of General Juan Velasco Alvarado

The dispute over oil exploitation prompted a nationalist general, Juan Velasco Alvarado, to overthrow Belaúnde's regime in October 1968. Suddenly, Peru had a de facto leader in uniform, who, unlike his predecessors, saw himself as a voice for the poor, installing what he called a revolutionary government. Shortly after Velasco's coup, the army took over the oil installations of the International Petroleum Company, offering no compensation to the company. The U.S. mining giants, the Cerro de Pasco Corporation and the Marcona Mining Company, were also expropriated, scaring away foreign investors. Velasco's regime moved more and more to the left. His most radical measure took place in 1969 when the general announced that Peru's old farms (*haciendas*), many of which belonged to the old Peruvian elite, were to be expropriated and transformed into peasant cooperatives. The agrarian reform, or *reforma agraria*, made Velasco a new version of the Latin American *caudillo*. His radical measures garnered great popular support among the Peruvian working class, but, in time, those measures proved to be disastrous. While Peru's old ruling class was dismantled, land productivity dropped, and the state-run cooperatives' inefficient management hurt the country's exports, eventually creating a huge foreign debt. By the early 1970s, the fishing industry had also been taken over by the government, and many private businesses were forced to have workers on the board of directors. This was followed by the government takeover of all newspapers and radio and television stations in order to create a large propaganda machine for the state.

Velasco's growing authoritarian rule was seriously undermined by the country's diminishing productivity. While his social reforms—doing away with the old Peruvian oligarchy and reaffirming the rights of the working and peasants classes—changed the face of Peruvian society, his administration lacked a sense of long-term planning, which led to economic chaos. In August 1975, Velasco was ousted by a more moderate group of officers who, headed by General Francisco Morales Bermúdez, swung to the right and implemented a number of difficult economic measures, which curtailed the purchasing power of the population significantly. In 1978, the government held elections for a constituent assembly with the participation of old and new political parties. APRA's aging Haya de la Torre was elected president of the assembly and charged with the task of writing a new constitution, paving the way for the country's return to democracy.

### The 1980s: A Difficult Return to Democracy

In 1980, Peru returned to civilian rule with Fernando Belaúnde's second administration. Belaúnde undid many of the military government's reforms. He also opened the country's markets to foreign investment and increased state spending to try to rebuild the country's infrastructure. However, lack of exports, economic disarray, and a growing foreign debt soon weakened possibilities for development. The 1980s also marked the beginning of a terrorist movement known as Shining Path (Sendero Luminoso), led by Abimael Guzmán, a university professor and former member of the Peruvian Communist Party. Attracting educated members of the Peruvian middle class, Shining Path's violent actions were ideologically based on the writings of José Carlos Mariátegui, who saw in communal Andean organization a base for socialism. Shining Path also assumed characteristics of both the peasant movement led by Mao Zedong in China earlier in the twentieth century and Peruvian peasants, sharing a philosophy of total destruction of the state to create a new society. Paying little attention to the rebels, Belaunde's government was slow to take any measures. But as the rebels' violent operations reached Peru's major cities, the army was asked to intervene. It was, however, largely unprepared for a guerrilla war. As Shining Path's war against the population grew, eventually leading to some 30,000 deaths and $25 billion in damage to the country's infrastructure, a second leftist movement, known as the Movimiento Revolucionario Túpac Amaru (MRTA), appeared in 1984. Allegedly financed by cocaine drug lords, the MRTA operated in the Amazon basin. Due in part to rebel insurgencies, by the end of Belaúnde's second term in 1985, Peru was hit not only by growing social violence, but also a strong recession, triple-digit inflation, and a $14 billion debt.

### Alan García

Meanwhile, a new political leader emerged: Alan García. After the death of Haya de la Torre in 1979, García was seen as APRA's new political hope. García's appealing youth and discourse appeared as an answer to the mistakes of the past and a bridge to modernity. He won the 1985 elections by a landslide, obtaining a strong majority in congress. His populist rhetoric proved effective during his first two years in office, but more difficult times lay ahead. Defying the International Monetary Fund (IMF), García announced that Peru would limit its foreign-debt payments to 10% of its export earnings, hoping that other countries in the region would follow his example. Soon, Peru's foreign credit was cut off, and by 1987 inflation reappeared as wages dropped dramatically. That same year, the decision to nationalize the banking industry in order to fight a deteriorating economy launched a major protest from many sectors of society, eventually forcing the government to revoke its decision. It also helped launch the political career of Mario Vargas Llosa, Peru's internationally acclaimed writer. More drastic economic measures were to follow, and by the time García stepped down in July 1990, Peru had experienced the highest rate of inflation in its history (the U.S. dollar, whose value in 1985 was sixteen *intis*, sold for 360,000 in 1990), along with widespread poverty and growing violence. García fled into exile in 1992, destroying APRA's longstanding image as a party of the masses.

### Alberto Fujimori

The unsuccessful governments of Belaúnde and García in the 1980s left great mistrust among Peruvians toward old-style politicians and political parties. Alberto Fujimori's victory in the 1990 elections confirmed that sentiment. The son of Japanese immigrants, Fujimori was a university rector with little experience in politics. His small party, Cambio 90, defeated Mario Vargas Llosa's Movimiento Libertad, a coalition of traditional conservative groups. Proposing a new style of independent populism, Fujimori attracted the vote of Indians, blacks, and other ethnic Peruvians, who saw Vargas Llosa as a representative of the old white elite.

Without a doubt, Fujimori dominated Peru's political scene from the time he assumed office. Despite his promises during the campaign, his government was forced to take drastic economic measures, raising prices and carrying out a currency devaluation that led to even greater hardship for most Peruvians. Still, his popularity remained strong as his government reorganized the economy, eventually curtailing inflation and obtaining new foreign loans. In August 1992, in a daring move against institutional democracy and with the army's support, Fujimori closed down the Peruvian congress in order to achieve stronger political control. He eventually called instead for the formation of a Constitutional Assembly, which his followers dominated by a large majority. This action received harsh criticism from the international community. But Fujimori's popularity at home received a great boost when Guzmán, the leader of Shining Path, was captured in September of that year, severely damaging the rebel movement. By then, Shining Path's brutality against political grassroot organizations had earned it countless enemies both in the cities, where many community leaders had been killed, and in the countryside, where peasant defense groups, or *rondas*, acted as a force against Shining Path with the support of the government. While at the present time, Shining Path has not disappeared, its activities are now few and isolated.

After Fujimori's many political victories in the early 1990s and modifications to the constitution, he was reelected in 1995. Despite his tainted legitimacy, he defeated Javier Pérez de Cuéllar, the candidate for Unión por el Perú (UPP) and the former secretary-general of the United Nations, in clean elections. Fujimori's party also won sixty-seven out of 120 seats in congress, strengthening his mandate and confirming the poor opinion of political parties held by voters. Many of them, such as Acción Popular and APRA, failed to receive even 5% of the votes.

The war against terrorism has left many scars on Peruvian society. In 1995, an amnesty law was passed to protect members of the armed forces of charges against human rights abuses since 1980. Hundreds of innocent people accused of terrorism charges by military courts remained in prison, while international pressure from human rights groups remained a constant problem for Fujimori's image. Yet violence remained as a constant concern in contemporary Peru. In December 1996, when the government announced the virtual disappearance of the MRTA, a group of its members blasted their way into the Japanese ambassador's home in Lima during a reception, taking hundreds of hostages, including members of Fujimori's cabinet. The MRTA's leader, Néstor Cerpa, insisted that he would liberate the hostages only if the government agreed to free 400 of his comrades from jail. The siege ended in April 1997 in a huge military operation in which seventy-two hostages were rescued by army commandos and all fourteen rebels died, including Cerpa himself.

In many ways, Fujimori embodied yet another version of the Latin American *caudillo*. His political power relied on the support of the military and a strong intelligence service, often accused of using its resources against members of the political opposition. Vladimiro Montesinos, a former captain in the Peruvian army and a close adviser to Fujimori, was the mastermind behind many intelligence operations. Although rarely seen in public, in the late 1990s Montesinos's image slowly deteriorated as he was linked to drug trafficking, bribing, and persecuting political enemies of the Fujimori administration.

So, despite Fujimori's popular election, Peru was far from being a full-fledged institutional democracy. Recent civil war and terrorism resulted in popular support for a one-man authoritarian rule, while the army continued to play a key role in the country's balancing of power. Furthermore, the Peruvian congress and the judicial system strongly depended on the will of the legislative branch of government. Fujimori called his regime a form of "direct democracy," portraying himself as a pragmatic technocrat and as a leader who spoke directly to his people. During the final years of his regime, Fujimori's economic policies resulted in a strong recession and growing poverty for many Peruvians; nevertheless, his well-publicized visits to shanty-

President Alejandro Toledo (2001). AP/Wide World Photos.

towns and rural areas confirmed his popularity and his one-man version of Peruvian democracy.

In April 2000, new elections were held with Fujimori aspiring to a third term in office. While to many voters he was the source of institutional continuity and economic stability for the country, it soon became evident to many Peruvian voters, and to the many international observers who oversaw the electoral process, that the government-run electoral machinery fraudulently reelected Fujimori. The main opposition candidate, Alejandro Toledo, the leader of Peru Posible, withdrew from the runoff against Fujimori (Peru's constitution requires that a candidate win over 50% of the popular vote in order to be elected president) and staged a massive campaign of protest against his opponent's authoritarian ways. Months later, as Fujimori's presidency deteriorated and a number of videotapes implicating Montesinos in corruption scandals became public, the president went into exile. In November 2000, Peru's legislature ruled Fujimori unfit to serve as president and Congress President Valentín Paniagua assumed office.

Paniagua called for new elections for April 2001. As political parties reorganized, Alan García returned in January of that year from a nine-year exile and unexpectedly threw himself into a race that most observers expected to boil down to a contest between former Congresswoman Lourdes Flores, the first woman ever to run for office in Peru. Surprisingly, Flores was defeated by García's APRA party in the first round. Finally, in a runoff election in June 2001, Alejandro Toledo was elected as the new president of Peru in a very tight race.

After ten years of an authoritarian government, Peru entered the new millennium testing its fragile democratic system once again.

## REFERENCES

Alden Mason, J. *The Ancient Civilisations of Peru.* New York: Penguin Books, 1957.

Alva, Walter, and Christopher B. Donnan. *Tumbas reales de Sipán. Ceramics of Ancient Peru.* Los Angeles: Fowler Museum of Cultural History, 1993.

Americas Watch. *Peru Under Fire: Human Rights Since the Return to Democracy.* New Haven, CT: Yale University Press, 1992.

Andrien, Kenneth. *Crisis and Decline: The Viceroyalty of Peru in the Seventeenth Century.* Albuquerque: University of New Mexico Press, 1995.

Basadre, Jorge. *Historia de la república del Perú.* Lima: Editorial Universitaria, 1983.

Baudin, Louis. *Socialist Empire: The Incas of Peru.* New York: Van Nostrand, 1961.

Bauer, Brian. *The Development of the Inca State.* Austin: University of Texas Press, 1992.

Bennet, John M., ed. *Sendero Luminoso in Context: An Annotated Bibliography.* Lanham, MD: Scarecrow Press, 1998.

Bowen, Sally. *The Fujimori File.* Lima: Peru Monitor Publication, 2000.

Cameron, Maxwell. *Democracy and Authoritarianism in Peru: Political Coalitions and Social Change.* New York: St. Martin's Press, 1994.

Cameron, Maxwell, and Philip Mauceri, eds. *The Peruvian Labyrinth: Politics, Society, Economy.* University Park: Pennsylvania State University Press, 1997.

Clayton, Lawrence. *Peru and the United States: The Condor and the Eagle.* Athens: University of Georgia Press, 1999.

Cock, Guillermo. "Inca Rescue." *National Geographic* 201, no. 5 (May 2002): 78–91.

Cotler, Julio. *Perú 1964–1994: Economía, sociedad y política.* Lima: Instituto de Estudios Peruanos, 1995.

Cotler, Julio, and Romeo Grompone. *El fujimorismo: Ascenso y caída de un régimen autoritario.* Lima: Instituto de Estudios Peruanos, 2000.

Crabtree, John, and Jim Thomas, eds. *Fujimori's Peru: The Political Economy*. London: Institute of Latin American Studies, 1998.

Degregori, Carlos Iván. *La década de la antipolítica: Auge y huida de Alberto Fujimori y Vladimiro Montesinos*. Lima: Instituto de Estudios Peruanos, 2000.

Del Busto, José Antonio. *Breve historia de los negros del Perú*. Lima: Fondo Editorial del Congreso del Perú, 2001.

———. *Francisco Pizarro el Marqués Gobernador*. Lima: Editorial Brasa, 1993.

Dobyns, Henry F., and Paul L. Doughty. *Peru: A Cultural History*. New York: Oxford University Press, 1976.

Donnan, Christopher. *Ceramics of Ancient Peru*. Los Angeles: Fowler Museum of Cultural History, 1992.

Gootenberg, Paul. *Between Silver and Guano: Commercial Policy and the State in Post-Independence Peru*. Princeton, NJ: Princeton University Press, 1989.

Gorriti, Gustavo. *The Shining Path: A History of the Millenarian War in Peru*. Chapel Hill: University of North Carolina Press, 1999.

Gunther Doering, Juan, and Guillermo Lohmann Villena. *Lima*. Madrid: Editorial Mapfre, 1992.

Hilton, Isabel. "The Government Is Missing." *The New Yorker*, March 5, 2001: 58–73.

Hudson, Rex, ed. *Perú: A Country Study*. Washington, DC: Federal Research Division, Library of Congress, 1993.

Jochamowitz, Luis. *Ciudadano Fujimori: La construcción de un político*. Lima: Peisa, 1993.

Kenney, Charles D. "Anti-politicians, Outsiders and Party Politics: New Conceptual Strategies and Empirical Evidence from Peru." *Party Politics* 4, no. 1, 1998: 91–109.

———. *Institutionalized Instability: Fujimori's Coup and the Breakdown of Democracy in Latin America since 1900*. South Bend, Ind.: University of Notre Dame Press, forthcoming [2003].

———. "¿Por qué el Autogolpe? Fujimori y el Congreso, 1990–1992." In Fernando Tuesta Soldevilla, ed. *La Política Bajo Fujimori: Gobierno, partidos políticos y opinión pública*. Lima: Fundación Friedrich Ebert, 1996: 75–104.

Lockhart, James. *Spanish Peru, 1532–1560: A Colonial Society*. Madison: University of Wisconsin Press, 1968.

———. *The Men of Cajamarca*. Austin: University of Texas Press, 1972.

Malpass, Michael A. *Daily Life in the Inca Empire*. Westport, CT: Greenwood Press, 1996.

Manrique, Nelson. *Historia de la República*. Lima: COFIDE, 1995.

Mariátegui, José Carlos. *Seven Interpretive Essays on Peruvian Reality*. Austin: University of Texas Press, 1985.

Markham, Sir Clements R. *The Incas of Peru*. Lima: Librerías ABC, 1969.

McClintock, Cynthia. *Revolutionary Movements in Latin America: El Salvador's FMLN and Peru's Shining Path*, Washington, DC: United States Institute of Peace Press, 1998.

McGregor, S. J. Felipe. *Violence in the Andean Region.* Assen, The Netherlands: Van Gorcum, 1993.

Morris, Craig, and Adriana von Hagen. *The Inka Empire and Its Andean Origins.* New York: American Museum of Natural History and Abbeville Press, 1993.

Murra, John. *The Economic Organization of the Inca State.* Greenwich, CT: JAI Press, 1980.

Neira, Hugo. *El mal peruano.* Lima: SIDEA, 2001.

Palmer, David Scott. *Peru: The Authoritarian Tradition.* New York: Praeger Publishers, 1980.

Palmer, David Scott, ed. *The Shining Path of Peru.* New York: St. Martin's Press, 1992.

Pease, Franklin. *Breve historia contemporánea del Perú.* Mexico City: Fondo de Cultura Económica, 1995.

Pozzi-Escot, Inés. *El multilinguismo en el Perú.* Cuzco: Centro de Estudios Regionales Andinos Bartolomé de las Casas, 1998.

Prescott, William H. *History of the Conquest of Peru.* New York: Modern Library, 1936.

Read, Jan. *The New Conquistadors.* London: Evans Brothers, 1980.

Rojas Samanez, Alvaro. *Los partidos y los políticos en el Perú: Manual y registro.* Lima: Asociación de Comunicadores para la Paz, 1983.

Rospigliosi, Fernando. *Montesinos y las fuerzas armadas.* Lima: Instituto de Estudios Peruanos, 2000.

Rudolph, James. *Peru: The Evolution of a Crisis.* Westport, CT: Greenwood Press, 1992.

Seligman, Linda J. *Between Reform and Revolution: Political Struggles in the Peruvian Andes, 1969–1991.* Stanford, CA: Stanford University Press, 1995.

Sheahan, John. *Searching for a Better Society: The Peruvian Economy since 1950.* University Park: Pennsylvania State University Press, 1999.

Shimada, Izumi. *Cultura Sicán.* Lima: EDUBANCO, 1995.

Someda, Hidefuji. *El imperio de los Incas: Imagen del Tahuantinsuyo creada por los cronistas.* Lima: Fondo Editorial Pontificia Universidad Católica del Perú, 1999.

Starn, Orin, Carlos Iván Degregori, and Robin Kirk, eds. *The Peru Reader: History, Culture, Politics.* Durham, NC: Duke University Press, 1995.

Stern, Steve, ed. *Shining and Other Paths: War and Society in Peru, 1980–1995.* Durham, NC: Duke University Press, 1998.

Stokes, Susan. *Cultures in Conflict: Social Movements and the State in Peru.* Berkeley: University of California Press, 1995.

Tamariz, Domingo. *Historia del poder: Elecciones y golpes de estado en el Perú.* Lima: Jaime Campodónico Editor, 1995.

Tauro del Pino, Alberto. *Enciclopedia Ilustrada del Perú.* Lima: Peisa, 1987.

Tulchin, Joseph, and Gary Bland, eds. *Peru in Crisis: Dictatorship or Democracy?* Boulder, CO: Lynne Rienner Publishers and the Woodrow Wilson Center, 1994.

Turner, Barry, ed. *Latin America Profiled.* New York: St. Martin's Press, 2000.

Vargas Llosa, Alvaro. *The Madness of Things Peruvian: Democracy Under Siege.* New Brunswick, NJ: Transaction, 1994.

Vargas Llosa, Mario. *A Fish in the Water: A Memoir.* New York: Farrar Straus Giroux, 1994.

Vargas Ugarte, Rubén. *Historia general del Perú.* Lima: Milla Batres, 1966–1971.

Varón, Rafael. *Francisco Pizarro and His Brothers: The Illusion of Power in Sixteenth-Century Peru.* Norman: University of Oklahoma Press, 1997.

Von Hagen, Victor W. *Highway of the Sun: Search for the Royal Roads of the Incas.* Plymouth, England: Plata Publishing, 1975.

Weiner, Raúl. *Bandido Fujimori: El reelecionista.* Lima: WWW Editores, 1998.

Zuidema, R. Thomas. *Inca Civilization in Cuzco.* Austin: University of Texas Press, 1990.

# 2

# Religion and Religious Celebrations

AS IN MOST Latin American countries, organized religion plays an important role in Peruvian society and culture. The Roman Catholic Church has enjoyed a privileged status in the state during most of Peru's history after the Spanish conquest. In the 1993 census, 88.9% of the some 26 million Peruvians identified themselves as Catholic. Despite recent social discontent regarding the conservative role and the clear participation of the Archbishop of Lima Juan Luis Cipriani in political events during the Fujimori regime, most Peruvians tend to feel that it is their role to uphold the tradition of the Catholic Church. At the same time, other religious groups have grown dramatically in importance in recent decades.

## HISTORICAL BACKGROUND

In the sixteenth century, the Spanish crown began working to solidify the Andean colonial order with the Church, to which it was tied by royal patronage. A priest, Hernando de Luque, accompanied Francisco Pizarro during the conquest of Peru in 1532, and many missionaries began the task of converting the indigenous peoples to Christianity. As a result, the Church came to play an important role in the acculturation of the natives, drawing them into the cultural orbit of the Spanish settlers. It also waged a constant war to extirpate native religious beliefs, but such efforts were met with only partial success, as the blended nature of Andean Roman Catholicism today attests. By the end of the sixteenth century, the Church began to accumulate important financial assets, particularly land, that would consolidate its po-

San Francisco Church, Lima. Photo by Gloria Satizabal de Araneta.

sition as the most important economic power during the colonial period. At the same time, it assumed the primary role of educator, welfare provider, and guardian of orthodoxy in the viceroyalty of Peru through the much-feared institution of the Inquisition. Despite problems of distance and slow communications, the partnership between the Catholic Church and the state endured through almost three centuries of stable rule and power.

Since the foundation of Lima by Francisco Pizarro in 1535, church activities have centered in Lima, with the cathedral and Archbishop's Palace symbolically located on the east side of the Main Square, or Plaza de Armas, next to the National Government Palace and the Municipality of Lima. The ceremonial functions of the state are blended into the rites of the Church, beginning with the inauguration of the president in the cathedral with high mass, Holy Week events, and the observances of major Peruvian saints' days and festivals.

Since independence in the early nineteenth century, the Church's power has slowly diminished, losing its exclusive control over education, maintenance of vital statistics, marriages, and the organization of daily life around church rites.

The constitution of 1979 marked the first official separation between church and state in Peru; nevertheless, the ceremonial aspects of the Catholic religion, its moral dictates, and its values are still deeply embedded in Peruvian culture. With priests and bishops playing active roles in local affairs in most communities, every village, town, and city has its official church or cathedral, as well as special religious days celebrated every year to honor a patron saint. These patronal festivals are focal events for reaffirming social identity and play important roles in the life of all types and sizes of community. Participation in these events is linked to religious devotions as well as political purposes. In many towns, there is a religious brotherhood, who is in charge of the organization of the festivity. Peru's largest religious celebration, the procession of the Lord of Miracles (Señor de los Milagros), takes place in Lima every October. During this time, the effigy of Christ is carried through the streets of the capital in an event that gathers thousands of faithful every year.

## RELIGION IN THE ANDES

In communities that maintain strong native cultural traditions, Catholicism is intricately mixed with facets of pre-Columbian beliefs and practices. The native populations hold firm animistic notions about the spirits and forces found in natural settings, such as the great snow peaks where the lords of sacred places (*apus*) dwell. The Incas and other Andean peoples worshipped the sun (*inti*) and earth mother (*pacha mama*) as well as other gods. In converting the people to Catholicism, the Spaniards followed a deliberate strategy of blending the faiths that was used throughout the Americas. Such an approach sought to substitute Christian saints for local deities, often using existing temple sites as the location of churches. Many of the biblical lessons and stories were conveyed through dramatic reenactments of those events at fiestas that permitted people to memorize the tales and participate in the telling. Thousands of Andean celebrations are built on such foundations.

The annual celebrations of village patron saints' days often coincide with harvest periods and are clearly a reenactment of pre-Columbian harvest observances combined with Catholic feast days. In many communities of the Andes, religious rites evoke natural and spiritual forces requiring sacrifices of animals, such as llamas or guinea pigs, the spillage of alcohol on sacred ground to maintain its fertility, or the burying of coca leaves and other natural goods to please the *apus* or the *pacha mama*. In numerous highland areas, the Spaniards introduced the custom of blood sports, such as bullfighting and other games of horsemanship, in which riders, riding at full gallop, attempt to ring the necks of fowl or condors. The contemporary novelist José María Arguedas evokes such practices in his novel *Yawar fiesta* (1941). In many ways, Andean religious practices conform to the sociocultural divisions of Peruvian society, with the Westernized coastal cities following Catholic practices inherited from Spain, and the Andean towns and villages reflecting the traditional belief systems, which endure as strong elements in modern practice and worldview. From the major celebrations, such as those of two Peruvian saints, Santa Rosa de Lima (1586–1617) and San Martín de Porras (1579–1639), to the dozens of revered saints, virgins, and crosses in village chapels, these feast days have a singular role in social life, bringing the population together in common devotion to the immortal figure of a saint or *apu*.

Throughout the many communities in the Andean region, the priesthood historically carried the colonial legacy in its dealings with the Quechua- and Aymara-speaking people in modern Peru. At the same time, nonprofit organizations, such as Catholic Relief Services, remained active in providing aid to many neighborhood organizations in poor urban communities. By the 1970s, however, a more radical social concern for the poor emerged in the Church in Latin America. Known as Liberation Theology (Teologia de la Liberación), one of its founders was the Peruvian priest Gustavo Gutiérrez. Gutiérrez's theological approach proposed a more progressive social role for the Catholic Church in peace and justice, especially among the poor. Gutiérrez reinterpreted traditional biblical and doctrinal themes highlighting a preferential treatment for the poor. Although Liberation Theology has generated considerable controversy, many of its central insights have been incorporated into official teachings under Pope John Paul II.

## OTHER RELIGIONS

Although the first Protestant group to come to Peru was the Anglican Church in 1849, Protestant groups as a whole remained largely marginal throughout the nineteenth century and the first part of the twentieth century. Since the 1970s, Protestantism has been winning converts in Peru at a relatively rapid rate, particularly among the urban poor. In the 1993 census, 7.3% of Peruvians were counted as Protestants, with the Church of Jesus Christ of Latter Day Saints (Mormons) forming about a quarter of the number and the rest belonging to various other groups. In many ways, the appeal of Protestantism is a reaction to the kinds of ceremonial obligations that have accompanied Catholic practices, as well as the failure of the Church to address adequately the pressing problems among the poor.

In Lima, the Evangelical Movement whose origins in Peru date back to the early nineteenth century, with an increasing influence since the 1980s, proved its increasing importance among the less fortunate: at the grassroots level, it was instrumental in organizing communal kitchens and self-supporting groups in poor areas of the city. Moreover, during the 1990 presidential elections, the church's popular organization was a crucial supporter of Fujimori's party, Cambio 90. During the campaign, the Catholic Church hierarchy felt threatened enough by the Evangelicals' support for Fujimori that it unofficially backed Vargas Llosa, an agnostic, against Fujimori, a Catholic. Several members of the Evangelical Movement later held government posts after Fujimori was elected in July 1990.

Much of the Protestant missionary attention has been directed toward the tribal peoples of the Amazon basin, where the Summer Institute of Linguistics (SIL), bible translators, and similar evangelical groups have long worked. The SIL has occupied a peculiar position in Peru through its long-running contracts with the Ministry of Education to educate the numerous tribes, such as the Shipibo and Machiguenga, and assist the government in developing linguistically correct texts for several groups. Nevertheless, nationalistic public reaction to the SIL's activities has provoked many attempts to force the organization out of Peru.

## SOME POPULAR FEASTS

The co-existence of pre-Hispanic rituals along with Christian celebrations best describes the many popular feasts that take place year-round in the various geographical regions of Peru. Such an example of what is clearly a case of cultural amalgamation between Indigenous and Hispanic cultures, another term used to refer to *mestizaje*, is illustrated in the Peruvian wooden craft (*retablos*) made by artisans in the highlands to represent a number of popular feasts. *Retablos* are usually divided into two levels: on the upper level, Andean and Christian gods dance, sing, drink, and enjoy lavish banquets, while on the lower level, humans imitate, to the best of their ability, the amusement of their gods.

Not a single day of the year goes by in Peru without a pre-Hispanic ritual or a patron saint being celebrated in some part of the country, dictated either by the local history of a given town or by the Catholic calender. These feasts take a variety of forms, ranging from pilgrimages, parades, or processions to local fairs or festivals. Of course, Andean festivities preceded the arrival of the Spaniards by thousands of years. Spanish conquistadors were both amazed and disgusted when, upon their arrival in Cuzco in 1533, they saw royal mummies parading among the Indian nobility and their servants, as if they were still living creatures. The Spaniards soon identified the notion of Takiy, a Quechua concept describing the singing and dancing that take place during indigenous festivities. While wind and percussion instruments predominated in pre-Hispanic music, the Indians were quick to incorporate new instruments brought by the Spaniards, such as the guitar, into their celebrations. By the same token, Spaniards involved in evangelization of the Indians used music and drama in their catechizing activities. Upon the arrival of Spanish missionaries between the fifteenth and seventeenth centuries, a number of festivities saw a unique blending of pagan and Christian features into their rituals. It is impossible to list the countless festivities that are still alive in Peru after many centuries of Hispanic cultural influence. Nevertheless, in reviewing some of the most important ones listed below it is important to keep in mind their multicultural origin.

### Señor de los Milagros (Lord of Miracles)

The procession of the Lord of Miracles (Señor de los Milagros), Lima's most venerated image, takes place through the city's downtown every October. This is the most significant and widely attended religious act in the capital during the year. The story behind this worship dates back to 1651, when a slave painted the image (popularly referred to as the Black Christ, or Cristo Moreno) on the wall of slave quarters in Pachacamilla on the outskirts of Lima. Soon the image reached Spain, inspiring a royal order from King Charles II, who referred to this American Christ as the Señor de los Milagros. In October 1746, when an earthquake devastated Lima, the wall with the image remained untouched. Soon thereafter, the faithful gathered for a mass to venerate the Christ and ask his forgiveness and protection. From that moment, the worship of this image began to spread among the inhabitants of Lima, and today millions of devotees pay their respects to the Christ. Countless miracles and favors are attributed to the sacred image.

In fact, the procession of the Señor de los Milagros, set in the tradition of many popular feasts in Spain, is a very powerful ceremony. The president of Peru and his cabinet, civil authorities, as well as people belonging to all social groups accompany the image on its rounds through the oldest streets of Lima. A number of brotherhoods take turns carrying the heavy litter on which the image is placed. The faithful usually dress in purple habits and make their entreaties surrounded by rising clouds of incense.

During the rest of the year, the image of the Señor de los Milagros is kept

Procession of the Señor de los Milagros. Photo by Gloria Satizabal de Araneta.

in Las Nazarenas, an old church in downtown Lima, where it is visited by its many worshipers. Around the church, merchants set up stalls and sell myriad religious items, as well as typical dishes, such as *anticuchos*, a dish of cubes of marinated meat similar to shish kebab, and *picarones*, a dessert shaped like a donut made of pumpkin and served with honey. Because of the procession, October is popularly referred to by Limeños as the purple month (*mes morado*). This month also marks the beginning of the celebrated Lord of Miracles Fair, or Feria del Señor de los Milagros, the oldest and most important bullfighting event in the Americas. Bullfights are held in the bullring known as the Plaza de Acho, first built by Viceroy Manuel Amat y Juniet in 1766, in the old district of Rímac. Some of Spain's most famous bullfighters have performed at the Plaza de Acho throughout the years.

### Holy Week or Semana Santa in Ayacucho

The celebration of Holy Week (Semana Santa) in the city of Ayacucho in the southern Andes is also one of the most traditional religious festivities in Peru, gathering many faithful who travel there for the event in March or April of each year, depending on the Catholic calendar. Although various processions and ceremonies take place beginning on the Friday before Palm Sunday, one of the most stirring celebrations takes place on the Wednesday before Easter. In the evening, Ayacucho's main square becomes a huge stage. The doors of the Church of Santa Clara open to the effigies of Jesus and Our Lady of Sorrows. It is a dramatization of the encounter between mother and son on the road to Calvary. The climax occurs when Saint Veronica approaches the Virgin, promising to give her news about her son. Mother and son finally meet in front of the School of Fine Arts. In a deeply dramatic scene, their respective litters are inclined to give the impression that the images are conversing during the procession, with priests offering incense on behalf of the people.

Holy Thursday is set aside for visits to churches and religious monuments. Ayacucho's bishop reenacts the humility of Christ, washing the feet of elderly faithful. Good Friday is a day for mourning the death of Jesus, and Jesus's traditional Sermon of the Seven Words spoken from the cross is symbolically preached in Spanish and Quechua.

Saturday is a day of rejoicing in the resurrection of the Lord. The traditional fair of Acuchimay is held on that day. Holy Week comes to an end with the arrival of Resurrection Sunday. At five in the morning the faithful receive the resurrected Christ as applause, and the pealing of bells and *huaynos*, a typical form of Andean music, and *marineras*, a festive form of music from the coast, are played and danced on the streets. The litter carrying the image of Christ is imposing: it is covered with hundreds of burning candles and carried by some 300 people throughout Ayacucho.

### El Señor de Qoyllur Riti or The Lord of Snow

The pilgrimage of the Lord of Snow (El Señor de Qoyllur Riti) is a moveable feast that takes place in May or June before the celebration of Corpus Christi in Cuzco. The sanctuary of Qoyllur Riti is situated on the ice-covered peak of Mount Qoyllur Riti in the Cuzco province of Quispicanchi. This ceremony is one of the most important manifestations of Andean religiosity. The festivity is the result of a mestizo liturgy, highly influenced by the Indian worship of the *apus*, or hills, mountains, and snow-capped peaks, and the spirits living in them, the Wamani.

To reach Qoyllur Riti, the pilgrims travel east from Cuzco for six hours until they reach Mawayani. After a night spent on the ground, the pilgrims, most of whom are on foot, rise early to begin the nearly five-mile hike to the top of the mountain. The trip takes about four hours, with rests at each of the nine crosses and shrines where the pilgrims pray and sing. At the entry to the esplanade of Sinakhara, at the top of the mountain where el Señor de Qoyllur Riti dwells, some 15,000 feet above sea level, the crowd stops to wash in the glacial runoff. This is considered a bath of purification, a prerequisite for entering a spiritual dimension in which the energy of the deities joins with those of nature and humans. Other groups from different villages, referred to as *naciones*, or nations, arrive with dancers and musicians at the site as fireworks begin. As thousands of pilgrims cover the hillsides and the plains, the many *naciones* (Qollas, Chunchos, Siqllas, Qara Chunchos), along with the Pabluchas or Ukukos (dancers dressed to represent alpacas and bears), cross the plains. In the morning the Pabluchas climb to the heights of the peak and cut blocks of ice to carry down. This is a rite of penitence through which they can attain their dreams of owning livestock, especially alpaca. Around the sanctuary, some pilgrims sell "dreams" and "wishes." They offer miniature houses, trucks, weddings, and trips. Buyers take their "dreams" to the sacred rock to be blessed by the gods, in the hope that they will come true.

The history of this festivity dates back to the late eighteenth century. The Catholic Church intended to gradually eliminate native religious manifestations and replace them with Catholic rituals. The result, however, was a mixture in which Christian worship coexists with the worship of the mountain spirits.

## The Virgin of the Candelaria in Puno

The feast of the Virgin of the Candelaria in Puno is one of the most important celebrations in Peruvian religious and musical folklore. Over 400 years old, it is celebrated every year on February 2 in the city of Puno and is, as the other celebrations described, a blending of pagan and Christian rituals.

The festivity has its origin in a mythical character named Anchancho. He represents the native spirits of the mines, the master and protector. In colonial times, the Indians would make him an offering and dedicate a special dance to him, a rite they later had to perform at midnight while the Spaniards slept. Through the offering and dance, the people ask Anchancho to allow them into his dominion, that is, the mine. When the Spaniards learned of the ceremony, they took advantage of it to encourage the Indian laborers to work in the mines. Abolishing old beliefs was not practical if the Spaniards were going to exploit the mineral deposits. The Indians' religious devotion increased as a result of this ancestral belief because Anchancho was the only god with whom they had contact while in the mine. Spanish priests who attended the ceremony saw it as a means of catechizing the Indians and so created a religious play to introduce to them the concepts of heaven, hell, and sin. It portrayed the angels' rebellion against God, led by the angel Lucifer, who was cast out of heaven into hell. As a result, the character of the Devil gained prominence, dressed in a mask, horns, and a tail in the many choreographed representations presented by the dancers who now take place in the celebrations. The blending of native and Western cultures gradually produced the Dance of the Devil (Diablada), the dancers' masks depicting the seven mortal sins.

The celebration of the Virgin of the Candelaria is, of course, the version of events in the Catholic calendar. Nevertheless, it is a colorful and vibrant feast on the shores of Lake Titicaca that attracts many visitors, as well as a number of musicians and dancers from the Altiplano area.

### San Juan or The Festival of St. John

In the jungle, the Festival of St. John honors Saint John the Baptist, who baptized Jesus and presented him to the people as the Messiah, according to the Bible. The festival is celebrated in a number of jungle towns and cities, including Iquitos, Moyobamba, Tarapoto, and Pucallpa, on June 24. One of the traditional customs during the festival is an outing to the river to swim and dig for nests of turtle eggs, an item the locals consider a delicacy for its taste and nutritional value. The traditional dish eaten during the festivities is called *juane*, a mixture of herbs, rice, and chicken wrapped in *bijao*, or banana leaves. Another part of the festivity is the ceremony of the Umsha, where celebrants dance in couples around a palm tree filled with gifts while trying to bring it down with machete blows. The couple who succeeds bringing down the tree is spiritually linked as *padrinos*, or godparents, and must prepare the Umsha the following year.

Overall, it can be said that the many celebrations that take place in Peru during the year, whether religious or not, are outlets for the creativity of the masses, who find in them a fitting stage for their music, dance, and numerous expressions of religious faith. The importance of these celebrations reflects the love of the people for rituals. As in any society with ancient customs, all public celebrations not only involve larger segments of society, they also allow for a sense of belonging in each community. And as the geographic scope of a celebration grows, so does the splendor.

## REFERENCES

Del Busto, José Antonio. *San Martín de Porras.* Lima: Fondo Editorial Pontificia Universidad Católica del Perú, 1992.

Fleet, Michael, and Brian H. Smith. *The Catholic Church and Democracy in Chile and Peru.* Notre Dame, IN: University of Notre Dame Press, 1997.

Gutiérrez, Gustavo. *A Theology of Liberation: History, Politics, and Salvation.* New York: Orbis Books, 1988.

Klaiber, S. J. Jeffrey. *La iglesia en el Perú.* Lima: Fondo Editorial Pontificia Universidad Católica del Perú, 1996.

Marzal, S. J. Manuel. "Categorías y números en la religión del Perú hoy." *La religión en el Perú al filo del milenio,* Marzal S. J., Manuel, Catalina Romero, and José Sánchez, eds. Lima: Fondo Editorial Pontificia Universidad Católica del Perú, 2000.

McCormack, Sabine. *Religion in the Andes.* Princeton, N.J.: Princeton University Press, 1991.

Merino de Zela, Mildred. *Pueblos y costumbres del Perú.* Lima: Munilibros, 1986.

Millones, Luis. "The Gods Dance, Sing, Eat and Drink and Mortals Too." *Calendar of Peru: Fiesta Times.* Lima: Unión de Cervecerías Backus y Johnston, 1998: 7–27.

———. *Una partecita del cielo: La vida de Santa Rosa de Lima narrada por don Gonzalo de la Maza, a quien llamaba padre.* Lima: Editorial Horizonte, 1993.

Millones, Luis, and Yoshio Onuki. *El mundo ceremonial andino.* Lima: Editorial Horizonte, 1994.

Mujica Pinilla, Ramón. *Rosa limensis: mística, política e iconografía en torno a la patrona de América.* Lima: Instituto Francés de Estudios Andinos; Fondo de Cultura Económica; Banco Central de Reserva del Perú, 2001.

Muñoz Monge, Antonio. *Folkore peruano, danza y canto.* Lima: Universidad Garcilaso de la Vega, 1991.

Peña, Margarita. *Theologies and Liberation in Peru: The Role of Ideas in Social Movements.* Philadelphia: Temple University Press, 1995.

Romero, Raúl. *Música, danzas y máscaras de los Andes.* Lima: Pontificia Universidad Católica del Perú/Instituto Riva Agüero, 1993.

Rostorowski de Diez Canseco, María. *Pachacamac y el Señor de los Milagros, una trayectoria milenaria.* Lima: Instituto de Estudios Peruanos, 1992.

# 3

# Social Customs

## TOWARD A MESTIZO SOCIETY

THE INTERMINGLING of different heritages that make up Peruvian identity today springs from the protagonists of Andean, Mediterranean, and European history. Each one has left indelible traces of its own creative vitality and intellectual achievements. The progressive fusion of these elements with each other, as well as encounters, whether in isolation or as a comprehensive hybrid, with the influences of other cultures, have given rise to a unique and quintessentially Peruvian identity. Of course, on an individual basis distinct characteristics manifest themselves due to different cultural influences and the landscapes that define different habitats. As a whole, however, this phenomenon is referred to as *mestizaje*, a Peruvian version of the concept of the melting pot in the United States in which all ethnic groups, along with their unique cultural traits, share a common social space, which forms the Peruvian nation.

In coastal areas of Peru, a large white population of European origin traditionally inhabited the country's most important cities, such as Lima and Trujillo, since the arrival of the Spaniards in the sixteenth century. Between the seventeenth and the nineteenth century, Asian and African groups also reached coastal cities and their influences continue to be apparent in present-day Peru. Such factors have traditionally separated the coastal inhabitant racially as well as culturally from his indigenous compatriots in the sierra. However, since the 1940s, the large-scale migration of Andean peasants to the main cities on the coast again transformed the ethnic composition of modern Peru.

The sea and the desert, the two distinct physical landscapes found on the coast, have a profound influence on its inhabitants. Sailors live in permanent contact with the sea, and the Peruvian coastline is one of the richest in the world. For years, farmers have worked persistently to cultivate the desert, which they fear more than the ocean itself, and make it a friendly living environment. The Peruvian farmer takes advantage of every last inch of the shoreline of the rivers, opens up new lands to cultivation by digging wells to channel underground aquifers, and dams creeks and ponds in order to make the unmoving sands flourish. Whether fisherman, farmworker, landowner, industrial worker, or simple employee, the coastal inhabitant is a courteous and receptive individual, with a great passion for games of chance.

In modern-day Peru, Lima remains an important symbol of Peruvian identity. A consummately Spanish city until the middle of the 1940s, when it became the nexus of the rural migrations (which also extended to a lesser degree but as intensely to other coastal cities such as Trujillo, Chiclayo, Chimbote, Piura, Ica, and Tacna), Lima would blend in the carefree and humorous temperament of its immigrants, the easy grace of its women, and the spiteful dry and biting humor common to all, the most identifiable and persistent characteristics of the coastal inhabitant. However, with its more than 8 million inhabitants, the majority of whom dwell in the shantytowns that radiate out from the more affluent core, Lima today reflects the motley faces of the country's ethnic mosaic, in which the inhabitants of Lima whose ancestors have lived in the city for over four centuries (Limeños) constitute a simple minority.

The intermingling of races in the Andean region has occurred with varied levels of intensity. The white population in cities such as Puno, Huancayo, and Cuzco is a minority and the mestizo barely manifests Spanish blood in a flowing ocean of Indian heritage. However, in Arequipa, Peru's most important city after Lima (at least before the impact of the peasant migrations to Arequipa originating primarily in Puno took place in the last two decades), the same process of ethnic blending had been more homogenous and has even witnessed a marked trend in favor of the Spanish side. Indeed, it has been the republic that has shaped the character of the inhabitants of Arequipa. Even though this city was the last to recognize Peruvian independence and adhere to the new democracy, it rapidly became the first to elaborate and defend those ideals. Arequipeños are people replete with contradictions: impoverished and proud, hardworking and religious, revolutionary and conservative, passionate and austere. Suspended 7,500 feet above sea level and located some sixty miles from the Pacific Ocean, their lives are hemmed in by a large number of volcanoes. Resembling the Mediterranean both geographically and in outlook, the inhabitants of Arequipa feel themselves to be

Women in the Peruvian highlands. Photo by Gloria Satizabal de Araneta.

neither part of the mountains nor the coast. Heir to Extremaduran and Basque sensibilities, there is no trace of the joy and liveliness characteristic of the Andalusians who populated Lima; nor is there the racial legacy and African rhythms of the coast, since slaves never came to Arequipa's lowlands.

If the heyday of the viceroys lives, endures, and draws to itself the spirit of the Limeño, the historical legacy of the Inca empire's splendor rivets the heart of the Cuzqueño. Surrounded by breathtaking scenery, ruins of stone that have resisted both the passage of time and earthquakes, and Baroque temples sculpted by Indian artisans whose techniques made their ancestral divinities glide across the surface of their work, Cuzqueños are both proud and reserved. They boast of the Spanish blood that flows in their veins, as well as their Quechua ancestry. Marked by a quiet and low-keyed temperament, Cuzqueños distrust outsiders and are both ambitious and rebellious.

The Puno inhabitants' spirit preserved nothing from Spain. Everything belongs to a remote past that is basically Aymara. Rebellious toward the Inca, their indomitable spirit did not collapse in the face of the Spanish conquest, and the Aymara continued to resist. Standoffish and alone at 12,000 feet above sea level, isolated by the landscape of the altiplano, they obeyed in silence until only a few decades ago the old Castilian codes of conduct that denied them the right to ride a horse or leave their immediate surroundings. Television, radio, and new modes of transportation have changed these peo-

Woman with llama, Cuzco. Photo by Gloria Satizabal de Araneta.

ple. Today, the Aymara range across the plateau on bicycle or any other means of transportation; they spill over the eastern and western slopes of the Andes, invading, just like all the other peoples of the mountainous zones, in search of new opportunities either in the cities of the coast or the highlands of the Amazon.

In the jungle, where the Jesuits and the Franciscans attempted to convert the natives to Christianity in the seventeenth and eighteenth centuries, the obsession with rubber impelled the colonization by precocious European adventurers and businessmen at the end of the nineteenth century and the first decades of the twentieth century. At the present time, the jungle remains the focal point for growing waves of Andean migration, and the process of *mestizaje* continues to forge a human archetype distinct from the other peoples of the Amazon. Nevertheless in spite of its separate origins, the jungle's inhabitants exemplify a Peruvian essence fundamentally linked with the rest of the country.

## TOWARD A DEFINITION OF PERUVIAN IDIOSYNCRASY

In spite of Peru's immense size and the diversity of peoples and customs that populate its territory, several centuries of interaction between different cultures and waves of immigration have endowed the Peruvian with certain general characteristics, the essence of which may vary from region to region, and even among social classes, but are further testimony to the idiosyncratic nature that separates and distinguishes Peru from other nations in Latin America.

One of these idiosyncrasies, ingrained fundamentally in the rituals of altar and state, is the love Peruvians have for ceremonial forms. The solemnity of official ceremonies headed by the chief of state, the hoisting of the national flag or the martial spirit of military parades, and, above all, the splendor of religious rites all manifest this propensity for the baroque. Both the Indian and Spanish legacies have contributed to this phenomenon. The chronicles of the Spanish conquest portrayed in great detail the pivotal role of ritualism in the pre-Columbian societies of the Andes. This was especially true in the Inca empire in which, because of its theocratic bent, the ceremonial symbolized the power held by the Inca as well as religion's importance in maintaining the empire. To a certain extent, this sumptuous exhibitionism was the downfall of Atahualpa, the last Inca, who, as witnesses to the event have related, appeared in Cajamarca in all his solemn imperial glory, thus facilitating his capture by Francisco Pizarro and his men in 1532.

To a certain extent, the regulations established by the Council of Trent (1545–1563), strengthening political and religious power between the Spanish crown and the Catholic Church, and remitted by King Phillip II throughout his possessions as laws of state, managed to take hold in Peru more than anywhere else in the Spanish empire. These structures demanded that bishops make every effort necessary to impart the Christian faith by means of paintings and other visual mediums. Consequently, the clergy felt obliged to adorn their churches and organize religious processions with the aim of glorifying adherence to Christian beliefs. This would begin a compulsive and meticulous wave of ceremonies in adoration of Christ, the Virgin Mary, and the saints that would last for the three centuries of Spanish rule and resonate throughout Peru. The Baroque period in the seventeenth and eighteenth centuries would witness the most far-reaching and sublime expression of these practices. Even today, these ceremonies organized by the regional elites still form the crux of the calendar year in most rural areas.

The Baroque flavor of these ceremonies would also impact the visual arts. In painting as well as architecture, uniquely Peruvian variations of Baroque art would leap forth, most spectacularly in the Cuzco school of painting and the mestizo architecture in southern Peru. These two phenomena, unique chapters in the art of the New World, achieved a remarkable fusion and synthesis and are a clear expression of *mestizaje*, where European and indigenous motifs overlap time and again. The many churches in Arequipa, the valley of Colca, and on the shores of Lake Titicaca offer further testimony to this marvelous eclecticism. The quality and originality of their decorative styles even manifested itself in the city of Potosí in present-day Bolivia, which has been one of the richest cities in the Americas since the sixteenth century because of its huge reserves of silver.

In addition to this love of ceremony and splendor, fatalism often drives the attitude of the average Peruvian. The forbidding terrain of Peru, bedeviled by earthquakes, unpredictable and sweeping changes in the weather (such the fickleness of El Niño on the Pacific coast), and the extremes of drought and flood, may explain this deterministic slant of the Peruvian psyche, as these forces are beyond human control. The predictability inherent in other latitudes is simply unknown in Peru's natural environment. This resignation may also stem from a cultural legacy: Peruvians were builders of sophisticated commonwealths in pre-Inca times and children of perhaps the most significant empire of ancient America, when Cuzco bent the entirety of the Andes to its whim. Later, under Spanish rule, Peruvians were exposed to the grandeur of the viceroys and were irrevocably altered by the deep transformations of material existence lasting from the middle of the nineteenth century well into the twentieth. Such changes compel the heirs of an ancient and sagacious people to accept the indisputable verdict of an all-encompassing fate. Certain traits of both Spaniard and Indian, coupled by the dictates of *mestizaje*, may also play a role in this deterministic view, given that the religious outlook of both peoples tends to flow in this direction.

Good-naturedness and ready hospitality are other qualities common to all Peruvians. The warm reception and pleasant treatment extended to visitors, the exemplary courtesy shown toward women, and the amenability to both friendship and revelry all testify to this ingrained kindness. Also significant are the Peruvian's loyalty to both family and clan, a sentiment deeply rooted in the threadbare existence of impoverished and marginalized urban slums, and a profound sense of solidarity with others, present above all in the popular movements rising out of the large-scale migrations from the country to the cities.

The historic meeting of ethnicity and culture that began in Peru almost 500 years ago resonates even more profoundly with the passage of time. The rural exodus from the highlands to the coast and the jungle continues the mingling of different peoples in modern-day Peruvian society. New technology allows for instant communications with any part of the country. Today, television sets are found even in the remotest areas, a development inconceivable only fifteen short years ago. Such changes help bring together disparate customs and attitudes, slowly making the distinctions characterizing the inhabitants of various regions less acute and allowing Peruvians from all walks of life to better understand and appreciate each other. In many ways, it could be said that Peru is a society in a permanent process of cultural synthesis.

The continual blending of people and culture has endowed Peruvians with a serene acceptance of their multifaceted legacy and, on a deeper level, allows for a reconciliation with its complex racial and cultural heritage. Despite many manifestations of racism found in Peruvian daily life (an unfortunate inheritance of Spanish rule), it is also true that Peru accepts its multicultural, multiethnic origin, and the state recognizes its duty to preserve and defend it in the constitution. *Mestizaje* is a point of origin whenever one begins to discuss the essence of Peruvian identity. It is also the destination to which one must inevitably return.

## CUISINE

Because of the arrival of many different peoples to its territory since the Spanish conquest, Peru is one of the world's gastronomic paradises, its food in many ways illustrating the process of *mestizaje*. In addition to a rich culinary tradition inherited from the Incas and their forebears, which is based on products that were domesticated in this region (potatoes, lima beans, and peanuts, among others), the Spaniards brought their own products, along with their Moorish slaves, some of whom married their conquistador masters and introduced the richness of the Moorish cuisine, especially sweets and desserts. Africans, who arrived soon after and were forced into slavery, came with their own gastronomic knowledge. And although this African legacy is not as rich in variety and products as those developed in the Caribbean region, Brazil, and the southern United States, it is present in some areas of the Peruvian coast.

After independence from Spain in 1821, Peruvian gastronomy was enriched by the migration of Italians from Genoa, Chinese from the province of Canton during the nineteenth century, who arrived to substitute for African slaves in farms and later in the construction of railroads, and Japanese, who arrived during the first part of the twentieth century. Other national groups that came in smaller numbers, such as the French and Germans, also helped create the mélange of Peruvian gastronomy. As a result, in modern times everyday food at Peruvian households is a mixture of national creole food, also known as *comida criolla*, and that of those countries mentioned above. It is not rare, for example, that a typical Peruvian dish such as lime-marinated fish, *cebiche*, be followed by a serving of fried rice, known as *arroz chaufa*, or a dish of spaghetti *al pesto*.

The Pacific Ocean off the coast of Peru, one of the richest in fish varieties, is a major determinant of the national cuisine. However, when speaking of typical Peruvian food, specialists normally agree that there are four basic gastronomic regions in the country.

### The Northern Coastal Tradition

This cuisine developed in major northern cities of Peru, including Tumbes, Piura, Chiclayo, and Trujillo. There are some common dishes throughout the area with small variations, like young goat cooked in a rich and spiced sauce, *seco de cabrito*, and a mixture of tender corn with garlic and onions, *pepián*. The farther north, the greater the variety of seafood that is available, especially seashells, of which the *conchas negras* of the Tumbes tidelands are considered a delicacy.

### Lima and the Central Coast Tradition

Constant migration to Lima from other parts of the country has made the city the place where all different regional cuisines meet. The cosmopolitan identity of Lima has also made it a place where an ample variety of international dining, including Indian, Argentine, Mexican, Japanese, and Arab fare, as well as most fast-food chains from the United States, are readily available.

Nevertheless, Lima's cooking has a definite local style of food. When in Lima, *causa* is a must. *Causa* is prepared with layers of yellow mashed potatoes mixed with olive oil, chili, and lime, and is usually accompanied by layers of prawns, shrimp, crabmeat, or fish, and a slice of avocado and hard-boiled eggs. Another very popular dish is the *lomo saltado*, a mixture of creole and Chinese dishes that includes small cuts of beef, onions, french fries, and chili pepper, or *ají*, and white rice. It is a common item in many Peruvian meals.

Chinese restaurants, or *chifas*, can be found all over Peru, but especially on the coast. The reason, as mentioned, was the arrival of Cantonese workers to farms and cities during the second part of the nineteenth century. Chinese Peruvians developed unique flavors by mixing meats with a variety of local spices, ultimately producing a cuisine that is difficult to find in other parts of Latin America. At the present time, Lima's old Chinatown, which was restored in the 1990s, hosts a large number of visitors on a daily basis.

### Andean Traditions

Rich soups are an old tradition of Andean cuisine in Peru. A variety of ingredients are used, especially in the meats used to prepare them (beef, lamb,

Varieties of dried corn. Photo by Gloria Satizabal de Araneta.

pork, goat, llama, alpaca, fowl, or guinea pig). These dishes are always rich in potato varieties (some 5,000 types of potato are available in the Andes), as well as corn and local herbs, and they go down well at high altitudes. Potato-based dishes can be presented in many different ways. Two of the most popular dishes are *papa a la huancaína* and *ocopa*, the basis of which is usually a yellow potato, known as *papa amarilla*, and a variety of spicy sauces.

Another novelty of Andean cooking is a primitive style of cooking, the *pachamanca*, which is as old as the inhabitants of the Andes themselves. To prepare it, a hole is dug in the soil, and stones are heated for several hours. The stones are then carefully placed inside the hole, with different kinds of meats and vegetables (lima beans, potatoes, and corn, among others) on top. A bouquet of aromatic leaves and pieces of cloth are included to protect the food. The hole is covered with dirt, and, after several hours of cooking, the food is ready to eat.

For lovers of spicy foods, Arequipa boasts some of the best in the country. A typical restaurant in this part of Peru is the *picantería*, known for its hot entrees. One such dish is *rocoto relleno*, a hot pepper of the *Capsicum pubecens* species, which is washed and boiled to decrease its spiciness and filled with ground beef and cheese. Also typical of Arequipa's cuisine is a thick, rich soup cooked with prawns called *chupe de camarones*. Both dishes are the pride of the local people.

## Amazonic Jungle Tradition

The most popular dish of the Peruvian jungle is the *juane*, a sort of tamale made out of rice and chicken and wrapped with *bijao*, or banana leaves, which give it its distinct flavor. Since banana leaves have to be fresh and do not grow outside of the Amazon basin, it is difficult to find good *juane* in Lima. For fish lovers, *paiche* (*Arapaima gigans*) is a wonderful choice. A white-meat fish that reaches over six feet in length, *paiche* is the basis for the best gastronomic preparations of the region, usually accompanied by manioc (tapioca), vegetables, or bananas. Another dish not found outside the area is the fresh palm (*palmito*) salad (*Guilielma ciliata*), called *chonta* in the jungle. Fresh *chonta* is not presented in chunks as is the commercialized canned version; rather, it is cut longitudinally to form what at first sight seems like a plate of spaghetti. *Chonta* is usually eaten as a salad with olive oil, vinegar, salt, and pepper.

South of Lima, the valley of Ica is Peru's vineyard. Peruvians are, more often than not, beer drinkers, and wine generally takes third place to the country's own version of brandy, the clear grape-derived *pisco*, the base of the frothy *pisco sour* cocktail. The drink was invented in the early twentieth century by the bartender at the Hotel Maury in downtown Lima and is one of Peru's most internationally known drinks. A very popular cocktail during social occasions, especially on the coast, *pisco sour* is a blend of lime juice, sugar, ice, and *pisco*.

In the *sierra*, a popular drink is *chicha*, a purple-looking beverage made out of dark corn. Its alcoholic version is *chicha de jora*, which is consumed during many festive occasions. In the jungle, a fermented drink made out of manioc, *masato*, is popular.

## REFERENCES

Alvarez, Isabel. *Huellas y sabores del Perú.* Lima: Universidad de San Martin de Porres, 1997.

Balbi, Mariela. *Sato's Cooking Nikkei-Style, Fish and Seafood.* Lima: Universidad de San Martín de Porres, 1997.

Custer, Felipe Antonio. *The Art of Peruvian Cuisine.* Lima: Ediciones Ganesha, 2000.

Fuller, Norma. "The Social Constitution of Gender Identity among Peruvian Men." *Men and Masculinities.* Vol. 3 No. 3 (2001): 316–331.

Guardia, Sara Beatriz. *Una fiesta del sabor: El Perú y sus comidas.* Lima: Ansonia, 2001.

Gutarra Carhuamaca, Jesús and Mariano Valderrama León. *Pachamanca: The Earthy Feast.* Lima: Universidad de San Martín de Porres, 2001.

Hocquenghem, Anne Marie and Susana Monzón. *La cocina piurana: Ensayos de antrolopología de la alimentación*. Lima: Instituto Francés de Estudios Andinos-Instituto de Estudios Peruanos, 1995.

Nugent, José Guillermo. *El laberinto de la choledad*. Lima: Fundación Friedrich Ebert, 1992.

Olivas Weston, Rosario. *La cocina en el virreinato del Perú*. Lima: Universidad de San Martín de Porres, 1998.

———. *Cultura, identidad y cocina en el Perú*. Lima: Universidad de San Martín de Porres, 1993.

———. *Cocina cotidiana y festiva de los limeños en el siglo XIX*. Lima: Universidad de San Martín de Porres, 1998.

Ossio, Juan. "Cultural Continuity, Structure, and Context: Some Peculiarities in Andean Compadrazgo." Raymond Smith, ed. *Kinship, Ideology and Practice in Latin America*. Chapel Hill: University of North Carolina Press, 1984: 118–146.

Salazar Bondy, Sebastián. *Lima la horrible*. Lima: Populibros, 1964.

# 4

# Broadcasting and Print Media

AS IN MANY Latin American countries, the history of the media in Peru is closely linked to the nation's political events. Along with the growing influence of television, radio, and, in recent years, the Internet, Peru's many newspapers and weeklies remain instrumental in the shaping of public opinion throughout the country.

## JOURNALISM

The printing press arrived in Peru in 1584. The first newspaper published in Peru was *La Gaceta de Lima,* which appeared in 1715. With the backing of the viceroy and the archbishop, it covered official news from Spain and Europe, along with some local news. It was later replaced by the *Diario de Lima,* which appeared on October 1, 1780, edited by Jaime de Bausate y Meza, a Spanish journalist who settled in Lima. Shortly after, on January 2, 1791, the members of the Sociedad Amantes del País launched the *Mercurio Peruano,* a magazine published twice a week that covered history, literature, and news. The *Mercurio Peruano* brought the new ideas of the Enlightenment to the colonies. One of its editors was Hipólito Unanue, a Creole, who would later be acknowledged as a scholar and would become one of Peru's founding fathers. The *Mercurio Peruano,* which never received support from the royal treasury, was last published in 1795.

The official daily *El Peruano* was first published in 1826. Organized according to instructions from Simón Bolívar, it remains in circulation today. The newspaper has changed names from time to time, but it has always published official news: laws, decrees, court notices, and judgments. Recently, it has expanded into a business newspaper, but without losing its official character.

### El Comercio (1839–   )

Peru's oldest and most respected newspaper, *El Comercio*, was founded in 1839, appearing as a single sheet printed on both sides with a manual press and bearing the title *El Comercio, business, political and literary daily*. Its founders were Manuel Amunátegui, born in Chillán, Chile, and Alejandro Villota, an Argentine. Amunátegui invented the "Communications Section" where, for a fee, any reader could publish opinions on any issue or person, usually under a pseudonym. During its early years, *El Comercio* distanced itself from politics and grew without major setbacks. In 1871, it supported the presidential candidacy of Manuel Pardo, which led the administration of José Balta to close the newspaper on June 6, 1872, prohibiting any newspaper to be printed on its presses. It reappeared on July 27, during the days of the uprising led by the Gutiérrez brothers that resulted in Balta's assassination.

In 1875, José Antonio Miró Quesada joined *El Comercio*. Born in Panama and brought to Peru as a young child, he had worked as a journalist for the newspaper since 1867. Amunátegui, who controlled the company, transferred his stock to his nephew, Luis Carranza, in 1875 in order to pursue other businesses, including the lucrative export of guano. That same year, Miró Quesada was appointed co-editor of *El Comercio* by Amunátegui, along with Carranza, but for all practical purposes it was Miró Quesada who ran the operation. By 1877, the company changed its name to Carranza, Miró Quesada & Compañía. Shortly after, Miró Quesada became the sole owner of the newspaper and began to participate in politics. President Nicolás de Piérola closed down *El Comercio* in January 1880 due to a critical editorial on alleged corruption in guano trading. The newspaper was again closed as Chilean troops entered Lima in 1881, only to reappear after the departure of the Chilean forces in October 1883.

Miró Quesada ran his company wisely, modernizing its machinery and operations and introducing foreign cable news service in 1884. *El Comercio* staunchly backed the Civil Party, which maintained a heavy influence on Peru's political scene during the various terms in office of Augusto B. Leguía, which ended in 1930. When Miró Quesada became president of the senate in 1901, his son Antonio Miró Quesada was appointed editor of the newspaper. In 1902, he installed the first rotating press in the country and, in 1904, the first linotypes.

In 1905, José Antonio Miró Quesada handed over complete management of the daily to his son Antonio, who was elected president of congress that same year and later president of the senate in 1918. On July 4, 1919, as a sequel to the election of Leguía as president of the country, a group of rioters assaulted the newspaper and a bomb exploded in the printing shop, destroying that day's edition. Two months later, mobs supporting Leguía attacked the paper's offices in dowtown Lima, setting it on fire. Antonio Miró Quesada, together with newspaper employees and typesetters, repelled the forty-five-minute attack with revolvers. In 1931, *El Comercio* backed the presidential candidacy of Sánchez Cerro, leading to a period of bitter confrontation between the newspaper and APRA, which opposed Sánchez Cerro. The political standpoint of the newspaper was nationalistic, conservative, anti-APRA, and anti-communist. The political rivalry between *El Comercio* and APRA resulted in more violence when, in 1935, an APRA fanatic assassinated Antonio Miró Quesada and his wife in downtown Lima, launching a longtime political animosity between the Miró Quesada family and Haya de la Torre's party in the twentieth century.

Shortly after Antonio Miró Quesada's death, his brother Aurelio became executive director of *El Comercio* and another brother, Luis, became chairman of the board. When Aurelio died in 1950, Luis took over the management of the paper in its entirety, continuing until its expropriation in 1974 by the government of General Velasco Alvarado.

Héctor Cornejo Chávez, president of the Christian Democratic Party but a staunch supporter of the Velasco regime, was named editor of the expropriated newspaper and quickly proceeded to dismiss from the company all members of the Miró Quesada family. Cornejo Chávez resigned when Francisco Morales Bermúdez replaced Velasco Alvarado in 1975. Cornejo Chávez was replaced by Helan Jaworsky and later by Alfonso Tealdo, two well-known journalists sympathetic to the military government.

With the return of democracy in 1980 during the second administration of Fernando Belaúnde, *El Comercio* was returned to the Miró Quesada family. Alejandro Miró Quesada Garland and Aurelio Miró Quesada Sosa became the paper's senior editors until the death of Aurelio in 1998. *El Comercio* continues to be the most respected and influential newspaper in the country and is justly referred to as the dean of Peruvian journalism. It continuously campaigns in defense of ecology and park preservation, and brings to light well-grounded claims on many domestic issues.

### *La Prensa* (1903–1974)

Another daily whose life closely reflects Peru's turbulent political life during the twentieth century is *La Prensa*. It was founded by Pedro de Osma y

Pardo, a member of the Democratic Party and a supporter of President Ni-colás de Piérola at the turn of the century. In 1905, *La Prensa* merged with *El Tiempo*, which was founded in 1895. Alberto Ulloa Cisneros, who owned *El Tiempo* and was already writing for *La Prensa* before the merge, became the intellectual mentor of the new daily. Ulloa continued supporting Piérola's party and opposing the Civil Party. In May 1909, *La Prensa*'s facilities were attacked and virtually destroyed. Its main editors, Leonidas Yerovi, Luis Fer-nán Cisneros, and Julio Portal, were imprisoned, along with Ulloa, who was later deported.

In 1915, Augusto Durand bought the daily and continued supporting the Democratic Party and opposing both the Civil Party's and Leguía's Demo-cratic Reformist Party. Intellectuals such as Enrique López Albújar, Abraham Valdelomar, Leonidas Yerovi, Alfredo González Prada, Alberto Ulloa Soto-mayor, and José Carlos Mariátegui wrote for *La Prensa*. In September 1919, shortly after Leguías's victory, *La Prensa* was attacked once again by govern-ment supporters, as was *El Comercio*. In 1921, the Leguía administration expropriated *La Prensa* and its director, Luis Fernán Cisneros, was sent to prison. Leguía appointed as editor the Colombian Guillermo Forero Franco, a personal friend of the president, who remained in charge of the daily until the fall of Leguía in 1930.

*La Prensa* stopped printing after the end of Leguía's administration, and, after several failed ventures, a group of businessmen headed by Francisco Graña Garland purchased the paper in 1946. In January 1947, Graña was murdered, the crime attributed to the APRA party. Pedro Beltrán Espantoso, an influential and wealthy businessman, took over the management of *La Prensa*, launching an intense campaign against the APRA and Communist parties, respectively. On February 17, 1956, toward the end of the Odría administration, government police seized *La Prensa*'s offices, detaining some forty people, including the editors and Beltrán himself. The following day, a group of reporters regained the facility, surprising the police. Odría soon authorized the paper's publication but exercised strict censorship over its content. The Sociedad Interamericana de Prensa, who had Beltrán as one of its distinguished members, criticized the government's order. Beltrán was freed thirty-three days later, and the newspaper started publishing once again.

During the second term of President Manuel Prado (1956–1962), Beltrán was appointed prime minister and minister of the treasury, becoming an influential politician. Later, during the leftist military government of General Velasco Alvarado in the 1960s and 1970s, *La Prensa* defended the interests of its agrobusiness shareholders against the military's Land Reform Law, which expropriated lands from some of the most influential families of Peru.

In 1972, Pedro Beltrán stepped down as editor of *La Prensa* as a result of a dubious interpretation of the government-supported Freedom of the Press Statute. He was succeeded by his nephew, Pedro Beltrán Ballón. In 1974, the newspaper was taken over by the military, along with all other dailies. Several editors sympathetic to the military continued to publish *La Prensa*, including Walter Peñaloza, an educator and diplomat, and Luis Jaime Cisneros, a respected university professor. After newspapers were returned to their owners in 1980 by the Belaúnde administration, *La Prensa* tried to regain its position as an influential newspaper, but, despite several attempts, it finally closed down in the 1980s.

### *La Crónica* (1912–1985)

*La Crónica* was founded by Manuel Moral, and its first director was Clemente Palma, son of the famed nineteenth-century writer Ricardo Palma. Its tabloid size and large number of illustrations were a novelty in Peru, but it was not a politically incisive publication and was of mediocre quality. In 1931, the millionaire Rafael Larco Herrera purchased the paper, apparently with the intention of participating in politics. But, in 1947, Larco Herrera transferred *La Crónica* to the Prado family, one of the richest in the country.

In the 1956 elections, *La Crónica* supported the candidacy of Manuel Prado, and its offices served as general headquarters for Prado's presidential campaign. Shortly after, the chairman of the board of directors, Manuel Cisneros Sánchez, was appointed prime minister and minister of foreign affairs for the Prado administration. The newspaper launched an evening edition called *La Tercera*, which achieved a large readership. In 1970, the Velasco government acquired the backbone of the Prado family's financial empire, the Banco Popular, which had fallen on bad times. Being one of the many companies controlled by Banco Popular, *La Crónica* was transferred to government hands. Its name was changed to *La Nueva Crónica*, and its quality improved in some aspects. In 1974, when all newspapers were expropriated by the government, *La Crónica* went back to its original name. Its editor was Guillermo Thorndike, an astute journalist and author, who made the paper an important political organ for the military. In July 1975, Thorndike was dismissed and replaced by Luis Gonzáles Posada, the brother-in-law of Velasco Alvarado. When Morales Bermúdez replaced Velasco Alvarado later that year as president of the country, the president of Banco Popular, José Luis Brousset, was appointed director of the newspaper. Due to poor management, *La Crónica* closed down a few years later.

### El Tiempo (1916–1930)

*El Tiempo* was founded and initially managed by Pedro Ruiz Bravo. The newspaper staunchly opposed the Civil Party, campaigning against President José Pardo and supporting Leguía, who was running as a candidate in the 1919 elections. José Carlos Mariátegui, César Falcón, and Humberto Del Aguila joined *El Tiempo* and dedicated themselves to defending workers' rights, such as lower cost of basic foodstuffs, improved living conditions, and reduced legal working hours. Thus, during its early years *El Tiempo* was a leftist newspaper. However, this trend went beyond the intent and political commitments of Ruiz Bravo, and Mariátegui and his group offered to buy the paper. In view of Ruiz Bravo's indecision, the group of journalists decided to withdraw and instead publish its own newspaper. Then, as a result of the general strike in Lima and Callao in May 1919, Pardo's government closed down the newspaper. Finally, *El Tiempo* identified itself with the Leguía administration and then disappeared once Sánchez Cerro deposed Leguía in 1930.

### La Razón (1919)

*La Razón*, founded by Mariátegui, Falcón, and Del Aguila in 1919, proved to be a great financial and physical effort for its founders. They used the archbishopric's printing shop, which produced poor-quality print. It came into print on May 14 and stopped on August 8. During this brief time, *La Razón* launched aggressive campaigns in defense of university reform and workers' rights. It closed as a result of pressure from the Leguía government against the archbishopric.

### La Tribuna (1931–1970)

*La Tribuna* first appeared on May 16, 1931, under the management of Manuel Seoane. As a channel for the APRA party, its objective was to promote the candidacy of Haya de la Torre against Sánchez Cerro in the 1931 elections. The APRA party enjoyed broad popular support, especially among working-class union members, and the newspaper was well received. Claiming election results had been tampered with in favor of Sánchez Cerro, *La Tribuna* launched a violent campaign against him. He then began to fiercely persecute APRA leaders and closed down the newspaper in February 1932.

From 1932 to 1945, during the governments of Benavides and Manuel Prado, *La Tribuna* was repeatedly reopened and closed down. Often it was published in secret editions, circulating from hand to hand among APRA members. In September 1945, after the victory of the Frente Democrático, a coalition that included the APRA party and brought José Luis Bustamante y Rivero to the presidency, *La Tribuna* reappeared, speaking in favor of APRA.

In 1948, after a failed APRA rebellion initiated by junior navy officers on October 3, the newspaper was closed and its staff jailed. General Odría, who took power on October 27 of that year, forced the APRA party to go underground. Its leader, Haya de la Torre, took refuge in the Colombian Embassy for five years, during which time *La Tribuna* remained an underground paper.

The paper reappeared in 1956, after APRA negotiated with Odría for its return to legality and supported the candidacy of Manuel Prado. Manuel Seoane directed the paper during this new stage. However, the newspaper was never able to compete with the major dailies, even though Seoane hired professional journalists, not politicians. Its pages did not cover much international news and mainly attracted readership among members of the APRA party.

After the victory of Fernando Belaúnde in 1963, APRA joined forces in congress with former President Odría and *La Tribuna* continued in the mire without major consequences, accumulating debts with the Banco Industrial due to loans approved through political pressure. In January 1970, during the government of General Velasco Alvarado, the newspaper was seized by the Banco de la Nación and the Banco Industrial, ending once and for all the troubled life of the APRA newspaper.

### Ultima Hora (1950–1992)

Pedro Beltrán Espantoso, editor of *La Prensa*, created a new company to publish this evening newspaper that became the most widely read evening paper in the history of Peruvian journalism. The tabloid combined sensationalist police news, extensive use of photographs, and the use of hoodlum jargon in its headlines. After it was expropriated in 1974, it was directed by Ismael Frías, and later by Francisco Guerra and Miguel Li Carrillo. When newspapers were returned to their legitimate owners, *Ultima Hora* repeatedly tried to regain its former position until it closed down in 1992.

### Expreso (1961–   )

*Expreso* was founded in 1961 by Manuel Mujica Gallo, a rich heir to coastal plantations with large interests in banking and the insurance industry. He entrusted the organization of the paper to the journalist Manuel Jesús

Orbegoso and later to Raúl Villarán. *Expreso*'s first managing director was the diplomat José Antonio Encinas del Pando. From the beginning *Expreso* was a successful paper, attracting both middle-class and working-class readers. In contrast to other papers, it had a workers' union almost from the start.

Along with Encinas del Pando, Efraín Ruiz Caro, a journalist and former congressman for the leftist Movimiento Social Progresista, was hired as editor-in-chief. *Expreso* was more liberal and independent than other dailies. It objectively covered the Cuban Revolution of 1959 and its aftermath and supported the 1962–1963 campaign of Fernando Belaúnde and, later, his presidency. In October 1964, the company launched the evening newspaper *Extra*, which reached a very high level of readership.

Mujica Gallo, *Expreso*'s main shareholder, was appointed ambassador to Austria and Turkey by the Belaúnde government and lived abroad, neglecting management of the paper. In 1965, Manuel Ulloa Elías, representing a large U.S. financial corporation and a group of politicians affiliated to Belaúnde, bought the newspaper and founded the company Editora Nacional, appointing Guillermo Cortez Núñez as its new managing editor. *Expreso* continued supporting the government of Belaúnde, and Ulloa, who grew increasingly closer to the president, was appointed minister of the treasury.

With the coup d'état of General Velasco Alvarado in October 1968, Ulloa was arrested and deported to Buenos Aires. *Expreso* launched a campaign attacking the military junta. However, its labor union, the Frente Unico de Trabajadores de Expreso y Extra, proclaimed its support of the Agrarian Reform Law issued by Velasco Alvarado's administration in June of 1969, a gesture that caught the attention and sympathies of his government. Efraín Ruiz Caro, at the time director of information for the agrarian reform, seems to have been the promoter of the expropriation of *Expreso* and *Extra* for alleged "public purposes" in March 1970 and their transfer to their respective labor unions.

The management of *Expreso* and *Extra* was entrusted to various members of the now defunct Movimiento Social Progresista, including Efraín Ruiz Caro, Francisco Moncloa, Humberto Damonte, and Guillermo Sheen Lazo, with the participation of Germán Gutiérrez, Augusto Salazar Bondy, and others, and later with the important presence of Alberto Ruiz Eldredge, a respected lawyer. The nationalistic and anti-imperialist politics of the Movimiento Social Progresista coincided with the politics of the Velasco Alvarado regime, and, consequently, the two tabloids became the military government's natural journalistic allies.

When all the newspapers were expropriated in 1974, Ruiz Caro was dismissed and replaced by Alberto Ruiz Eldredge, who resigned before a year had gone by and was replaced by the educator Leopoldo Chiappo. Under

Chiappo's management, *Expreso* became completely independent of the government. The paper harshly criticized the Morales Bermúdez government for the deportation in August 1975 of journalists and labor leaders who opposed the military regime, and of APRA politicians. In 1976, Chiappo was dismissed and replaced by Juan José Vega, a historian and former university professor who was sympathetic to the politics of the second phase of the military government. In 1980, when Belaúnde was elected president once again, his administration returned *Expreso* and *Extra* to Manuel Ulloa. At the present time, *Expreso* remains in circulation but its credibility among the public has decreased considerably due to its support of the Fujimori regime in the 1990s.

### Correo (1962–1982)

*Correo* was founded by Luis Banchero Rossi, a successful fishing industry tycoon who in ten years had created a financial empire based on fishmeal manufacture. Banchero Rossi represented the interests of the already powerful Sociedad Nacional de Pesquería. He created the Empresa Periodística Nacional, which edited the newspaper *Sur*, later changing its name to *Correo*, in the southern city of Tacna, in addition to other newspapers with the same name in Arequipa, Huancayo, and Piura. The *Lima Correo* was directed by Raúl Villarán, Mario Castro Arenas, and Roberto Ramírez del Villar. The company created the sensationalist paper *Ojo*, which, though a morning edition, had the characteristics of an evening paper and at times reached a circulation of more than 200,000. *Ojo* continues to be published, enjoying ample readership.

In January 1972, Banchero was mysteriously murdered, and his relatives inherited the company. In July 1974, it was expropriated by the Velasco Alvarado regime. On February 5, 1975, the paper's headquarters were attacked and burned by mobs loyal to the government. For several weeks, the paper was printed at *La Prensa*'s printing presses, until a modern rotating press was purchased with insurance money. The newspaper was returned to its owners by Belaúnde, but, after several recovery attempts, it closed down in 1982.

### La República (1981–   )

*La República* was created in 1981 and first headed by Carlos Maraví Gutarra and Gustavo Mohme. Its first managing directors were Guillermo Thorndike and Alejandro Sakuda Moroma. It was one of the newest newspapers to be founded after the older newspapers were returned to its original owners in 1980 by the Belaúnde administration and the return to democratic rule in Peru. From the beginning to the present, it has adopted a critical attitude toward the various governments in office.

### Outlook

Political identification of newspapers with a particular party or government has diminished in the past few years, reflecting the general lack of interest in politics pervasive in the country. In addition, the speed with which domestic and world news is transmitted through television has become serious competition for most dailies. As a result, their circulation has dropped significantly. Nevertheless, more than fifteen newspapers are currently published in Lima, including *El Peruano*, the government's official newspaper.

Some newspapers are published in the major departmental capitals, in competition with the Lima newspapers and television. The most important are *El Pueblo* and *Correo* in Arequipa; the 100-year-old *La Industria* in Trujillo and Chiclayo; *El Tiempo* and *Correo* in Piura; *El Sol* in Cuzco; *La Voz* and *Correo* in Tacna; and *Correo* in Huancayo.

### MAGAZINES

Many magazines also enjoy wide readership in Peru and continue to be important sources of political and cultural analysis. Among the most important ones are *Caretas*, a weekly founded in 1950 and currently directed by Enrique Zileri Gibson, one of Peru's most respected journalists; *Debate*, a bimonthly edited by Augusto Alvarez Rodrich; and *Quehacer*, a bimonthly directed by Abelardo Sánchez León and published since 1965 by the Centro de Estudios y Promoción del Desarrollo (DESCO), a social sciences think tank and research organization in Peru.

### RADIO

Radio broadcasting did not arrive in Peru until 1925, when President Augusto B. Leguía inaugurated the first radio station, the Peruvian Broadcasting Company. A one-and-a-half-watt transmitter and two sixty-five-foot towers were used for the first broadcast. An amazed crowd listened to the first transmission through speakers installed in the Plaza de Armas and the Plaza San Martín in downtown Lima.

Radio broadcasting had been popular in the United States since 1920 and in France and Germany since 1921. In South America, Argentina was the first country to broadcast through radio waves. In Peru, the acronym OAX began to sound familiar to radio listeners. The Peruvian Broadcasting Company was renamed Radio Nacional in 1925. Then Radio Grellaud appeared (later known as Radio Lima), as did Radio Dusa. In 1935, Radio Miraflores, Radio Internacional, and Radio Goycochea went on the air. That same year, radios began selling commercially in Peru, becoming a popular household item.

Advertising discovered an effective publicity medium in radio, and the first spoken news and editorials were born. Variety artists and theater actors found a new source of work, and a new literary genre was born: the radio soap opera. Using the waves of Radio Dusa, three restless young men, César Miró, Augusto Mariátegui Oliva, and José Torres Vidaurre, created in 1936 the first journalistic program, *La Revista Oral.* This program called a protest demonstration against the Nazis who forced the unfair withdrawal of the Peruvian soccer team from the Berlin Olympics in 1936. Of the ten stations existing by 1937, only five still existed by 1941: Radio Internacional, Radio Goycochea (later named Radio Central), Radio Miraflores, Radio Nacional, and Radio Lima. Radio América and Radio Mundial opened in 1942, followed by Radio Colonial, later known as Radio La Crónica, which jointly popularized shows before a live radio-hall audience with Radio Victoria. Radio El Sol and Radio Panamericana went on the air in the 1950s.

## Radio Stars

Starting in the mid-1930s, radio stars gained fame, including Edmundo Moreau, Teresita Arce, known as "Chola Purificación," "Cholo" Rebolledo, Paco Andreu, Antonia Puro, Alex Valle, Juan Malborg, Ernestina Zamorano, and the musicians Lucho de la Cuba and Filomeno Ormeño. Well-known for their talent with creole music were a young singer with a gentle voice called Jesús Vásquez, Alicia Lizárraga, Juan Criado, the trio Los Trovadores del Perú, the duo La Limeñita y Ascoy, and Eloísa Angulo. Other popular singers included Roberto Tello, the tango singer Raúl del Mar, and Aurelio Collantes. The contribution of imaginative scriptwriters such as Jorge Rivarola, Carlos Ego Aguirre, Queca Herrero, César Miró, and others made the radio soap opera a popular genre through daily airings of world theater and other literary adaptations. The first radio-theater leading man, the father of soap operas, was Guillermo Lecca. Other admired voices were those of actors such as Elvira Travesí, Gloria Travesí, Elvira Tizón, Consuelo Rey, Pepe Muñoz, and the Ureta Zamorano brothers, among others.

The greatest soap opera success in the 1950s was *El Derecho de Nacer* (The Right to Be Born), with popular actors such as Mario Rivera, Pablo Fernández, Lucía Irurita, Javier del Solar (Albertito Limonta), Roberto Vargas, and the "villain" Carlos Ego Aguirre. Comic programs such as *Loquibambia* (A Crazy World), and *Escuelita Nocturna* (School by Night), with the Argentinean Freddy "the Grouch," became the rage. Aired live, these comic programs topped the ratings and included distinguished cast members such as comedians "Chicho" Gordillo, Piero Solari, Carlos Onetto "Pantuflas," Felipe Sanguinetti, and a young country bumpkin, Tulio Loza.

Musical performances packed theaters and were transmitted to thousands of homes, featuring such prominent artists as Imperio Argentina, Ima Súmac, Hugo del Carril, Libertad Lamarque, José Mojica, Jorge Negrete, Pedro Infante, "Tin Tan," Mario Moreno "Cantinflas," Lucho Gatica, and Dámaso Pérez Prado. This was the golden age of radio, when the audience attended radio halls as a common social event.

Radio shows could not be complete without the emotion brought by Peru's own "minstrels," musical stars who themselves filled the halls. Peruvian creole music was never more popular than with the voices and guitars of true idols such as Los Embajadores Criollos, Los Trovadores del Perú, Los Morochucos, Irma and Oswaldo, the young Troveros Criollos featuring Jesús Vásquez, Esther Granados, the "Cholo" Luis Abanto Morales, Roberto Tello, and Raúl del Mar.

With soccer as the leading sport in Peru, sports programs became broadcasting role models and an important part of Peruvian popular culture beginning in the early part of the twentieth century. Such is the case of *Pregón Deportivo*, produced and hosted by the journalist Oscar Artacho, as well as the program *Ovación*, originally hosted by Alfonso "Pocho" Rospigliosi, one of Peru's most popular sports broadcasters. Pocho passed on in the 1980s, but his son Micky continued where he left off. In horse racing, also a popular sport in Peru, the voice of the euphoric Augusto Ferrando was enormously popular with audiences from around the country.

### Radio Today

Times have changed considerably for radio in Peru. With thirty-five AM and twenty-four FM stations, the Lima and Callao dial is crowded, despite powerful transmitters and satellites. Radio soap operas have practically disappeared, replaced by television soap operas. Most radio programs merely play music and address a very young audience, influenced by international record companies. Radio stations produce popular music idols promoted by record and television companies. Some FM stations do air very high-quality classical music programs with very little advertising. One radio chain transmitter, Radioprogramas del Perú, airs news from various points in the country, with nationwide coverage, and deservedly has a very large audience.

Radio is also extensively used for educational purposes, mostly by religious groups.

Radio stations exist in every major city or urban area, playing an important role in integrating the country's difficult geography. In some remote places, like the Amazonian departments of Loreto, Ucayali, Madre de Dios, Amazonas, and San Martín, radio takes on the functions of both the press and the mail. It is often used for specific purposes such as making family announcements or reporting on commercial river traffic.

## TELEVISION

Television was initially used in Peru for educational and cultural purposes. In 1957, United Nations Educational, Scientific and Cultural Organization (UNESCO) donated television transmission equipment to the Ministry of Education to help train professionals and technicians in the use of this new technology.

In January 1958, the first black-and-white transmissions began with documentary films on Channel 7 that were broadcast from studios in the Ministry of Education. Because there were few TV receivers in Lima, coupled with the technical difficulties of initial transmissions, the programs elicited little response or interest from the public. Channel 7 continues to broadcast with modern equipment as the only government channel, but its ratings remain low.

By late 1958, commercial television began with the launching of Channel 4, owned by Compañía Peruana de Radiodifusión, operated by Radio América. The initial partners were Guillermo Ureta, Iván Blume, Jesús Antonio Umbert, José Bolívar, and Jorge Carcovich. They had very little capital to invest, but once Nicanor Gonzales Vásquez, a local entrepreneur, joined in, his negotiating skills attracted the necessary capital to build the company.

In August 1959, Compañia Peruana de Producciones Radiales y Televisión aired the second commercial signal through Channel 9. This company was financially linked to Radio El Sol and the newspaper *El Comercio.*

The third commercial television station in the country, Panamericana Television, later known as PANTEL, aired in October 1959 on Channel 13. The company was founded by Genaro Delgado Brandt, his sons Genaro, Héctor, and Manuel Delgado Parker, and others. Delgado Brandt owned Radio Central and later bought Radio Panamericana. From the beginning, Channel 13 was well managed and topped the ratings. The company benefited from the guidance given by the Cuban Goar Mestre, who owned television stations in various countries and was connected to the Columbia Broadcasting System (CBS). In January 1963, the Channel 13 frequency band was changed to Channel 5, which had been initially reserved for operation by the government. Its closeness on the dial displeased the owners of Channel 4. To prevent the abandoned Channel 13 from landing in the hands of competitors, Panamericana Televisión-Asociación de Fomento Cultural was simultaneously established. This company obtained Channel 13 and delivered it through a joint operation agreement to Universidad de Lima to be used by its new Communication Sciences Department. Channel 13 stopped broadcasting in 1974. Channel 5, which is currently part of the PANTEL group, is a leading national television station in Peru.

In May 1962, the company Radiodifusora Victoria aired on Channel 2. Its owners were the brothers José Eduardo, Oscar, and Jaime Cavero Andrade, who also owned a radio station chain. This channel stopped transmitting in 1972 and eleven years later was transferred to Compañia Latinoamericana de Radiodifusión under the name Frecuencia 2. Also in 1962, Antonio Umbert started Radio Televisión Continental, Channel 6, in the city of Arequipa, which was linked to Channel 4 in Lima.

In November 1967, Bego Televisión, founded by the Belmont group, which also owned Radio Excelsior, Radio Atalaya, and Radio 1160, launched the signal for a new television channel, Channel 11. It failed to attract a large viewing audience at first, but years later, upon the initiative of broadcaster Ricardo Belmont, a public offering of shares to recapitalize his TV station RBC Televisión attracted 150,000 small shareholders.

In 1971, the military government of General Velasco Alvarado issued the General Telecommunications Law, allowing government intervention in television as well as in other mass communications media. This, in practical terms, permitted the government to expropriate 51% of television company shares. The volume of advertising was reduced and programs produced in Peru were promoted, stressing educational programs.

The return to democracy in 1980 dismantled the system created by the military government, which had brought about technical and creative stagnation in Peruvian television. In March 1980, color television programming began. And when Fernando Belaúnde assumed office for his second term in August of 1980, the television broadcasting companies were returned to their owners. This action was accompanied by a series of additional benefits that allowed the companies to consolidate and make nationwide coverage a reality.

In 1987, Channel 8, owned by the Compañia de Radiodifusión Arequipa, appeared in Arequipa, and in 1989, Empresa Radiodifusora 1160 starting airing its signal on Channel 13, Global Televisión.

In 1992, President Alberto Fujimori initiated his free market policy, allowing any foreign company to invest in domestic companies, including communications companies, which had been forbidden up to that time. The

Compañía Peruana de Radiodifusión, Channel 4, then proceeded to sell 61% of its stock to the powerful Mexican conglomerate Televisa. In 1995, the PANTEL group, owner of Panamericana Televisión, Channel 5, began trading stocks and bonds in the international market.

Currently, the main channels cover almost the entire Peruvian territory, thanks to satellites and the creation of nationwide affiliates. In some areas of the country, there are small community organizations and other nonprofit organizations that broadcast television signals for limited periods during the day.

In 1983, the first cable closed circuit channel was established in the Amazon city of Iquitos. A parabolic antenna captured programming from some thirty foreign channels, rebroadcasting it to its affiliates. In 1989, the company Telecable began operating, offering cable television for the first time in Lima. In the 1990s, the Telefónica Group, a Spanish multinational, opened a second cable system known as Cablemágico. In Arequipa, cable service has been provided by the company Cable Star since 1990.

Peruvian television is very similar to that of most Latin American countries, where quality and programming is subject to advertising, which promotes mass-consumption products. Except for Channel 7, all stations are private ventures and programming depends on ratings. Of the $200 million spent annually on advertising in Peru, about 70%, some $140 million, is invested in television advertising. As a whole, television has become increasingly powerful because of its influence on public opinion, far greater than that of the written press.

## REFERENCES

Alegría, Alonso. *OAX: Crónica de la radio en el Perú (1925–1980)*. Lima: Radioprogramas Editores, 1988.

Alfaro Moreno, Rosa María. *Cultura de masas y cultura popular en la radio peruana.* Lima: Tarea, 1990.

Durand, José, ed. *La Gaceta de Lima. Volume I: 1756–1762: De Superunda a Amat.* Lima: Cofide, 1982.

———. *La Gaceta de Lima. Volume II: 1762–1765: Apogeo de Amat.* Lima: Cofide, 1982.

Gargurevich, Juan. *Los periodistas.* Lima: La Voz Ediciones, 1999.

———. *Historia de la prensa peruana.* Lima: La Voz Ediciones, 1991.

———. *Comunicación y democracia en el Perú.* Lima: Editorial Horizonte, 1989.

———. *Introducción a la historia de los medios de comunicación en el Perú.* Lima: Editorial Horizonte, 1977.

———. *Prensa, Radio y TV: Historia crítica.* Lima: Editorial Horizonte, 1987.

Geddes, Henry William. *Television in Peru: Industry and Cultural Form.* Ph.D. dissertation, University of Texas at Austin, 1989.

Mendoza Michelot, María. *Inicios del periodismo en el Perú.* Lima: Universidad de Lima, 1997.

Pretell Lobatón, Josué. *Visión histórica de la televisión en el Perú.* Lima: Osimandia, 1987.

Vich, Víctor. "Imaginario popular en la parodia política: Hacia un estudio del humor en la televisión peruana." *Debates en Sociología* 18 (1993): 263–292.

Vivas, Fernando. *En vivo y en directo: Una historia de la televisión en el Perú.* Lima: Universidad de Lima, 2001.

Wood, David. "The Peruvian Press under Recent Authoritarian Regimes, with Special Reference to the Autogolpe of President Fujimori." *Bulletin of Latin American Research* 19 (2000): 17–32.

Zanutelli Rosas, Manuel. *Guía biográfica del periodismo peruano.* Lima: INIDE, 1989.

# 5

## Literature

TO SPEAK OF a national literature in Peru is to suggest the existence of a body of writing based on the identification of the nation's historical coherence, unity of language, national goals, social awareness, and cultural identity. This concept is problematical in the case of Peru, given the country's geographical, racial, cultural, and historical diversity. To date, in the ongoing work to identify a national literary canon for Peru, historical approaches have dealt primarily with learned texts in Spanish and little with popular literature. Indigenous literature written in Quechua and other ethnically based literatures have been looked at primarily from anthropological viewpoints for their testimonial value. The project for the future will be to incorporate all literary strata—dominant and popular, written and oral—to appreciate "Peruvian" literature in all its multiplicity and diversity.

When the Spaniards arrived in Peru, the Inca empire was in an expansionist stage and had already extended its boundaries far beyond what we know today as Peru. While Inca pictographic art, ceramics, jewelry, and cloth provide highly valuable insights into their history, a knowledge enriched by the role of the state's statisticians who kept precise mathematical records on sets of abacuslike colored strings with knots, Inca literary production was not recorded in writing but instead was orally transmitted from one generation to the next. The state's wise men were responsible for documenting official history in this fashion, just as anonymous community bards would compose lyric poetry and songs that were geared toward expressing feelings and sentiments dealing with planting and harvest, family celebrations, and events related to daily trials and tribulations. These more intimate and personal compositions dealt with pastoral, sentimental, and erotic love themes. Another indigenous form of poetic composition that was sung and danced to is the *huayno*. In order to keep traditions intact and thus safeguard a unified, centralized theocracy, the wise men also created epic poetry to celebrate the Inca empire's origins. Such is the case for the legend of Manco Cápac and Mama Ocllo, who appear near Lake Titicaca and later make Cuzco the capital of the Inca empire. The statisticians would maintain a living memory of these heroic deeds, and later, after the conquest, the Spanish priests, through their knowledge of the vernacular languages, would preserve fragments of these compositions in their chronicles.

While rich in its own oral literary material such as proverbs, fables, and stories, as well as in song, dance, and spectacle, Inca society underwent significant transformation with the arrival of the Spaniards. In 1525, Charles V mandated Spanish as the official language in Peru and ordered Indian leaders to learn it. The influence of Spanish can be observed in two ways at this early stage of the conquest: first, as grassroots speech based on popular expressions and songs, ballads, and poetry that are tied to historical events; and second, as an erudite, civilized, written language cultivated by intellectuals and nobles to demonstrate the linguistic splendor of the Spanish Golden Age. A third ingredient that further transforms the literature produced in this part of the Americas is the incorporation of Quechua, Aymará and their dialects into this new Spanish language. And so begins five centuries of painful transculturation.

## THE CONQUEST AND COLONIAL PERIOD: THE SIXTEENTH, SEVENTEENTH, AND EIGHTEENTH CENTURY

During the first two centuries after the conquest, Quechua-derived but Hispanic-influenced dramatic productions assimilated the world of the indigenous nobility to Western literary tradition. An example is *El pobre más rico* (The Richest Poor Man Around), published in the seventeenth century by Gabriel Centeno de Osma, structured on the *auto sacramental*, a eucharistic play popular in Spain, showing similarities with later European drama, and written in Quechua. Also important is the play *El hijo pródigo* (The Prodigal Son), the authorship of which is attributed to Juan de Espinosa Medrano (1629–1688), known as *El Lunarejo*. This play is a religious allegory with antecedents in native drama. It uses Quechua and Spanish, creating a unique Cuzco dialect. But by far the best-known colonial drama is *Ollantay*, its origin still highly contested. With thematic antecedents in pre-Columbian culture, the play's style, structure, and characters make it reminiscent of

Spanish Golden Age theater. It is commonly believed that this form of theater provided the impetus for creating postconquest, anti-European indigenous dance and drama spectacles that can still be seen in contemporary indigenous choreography.

The problems regarding cultural origin and authorship of indigenous literature, before and after the Spanish conquest, are best seen in the controversy surrounding *Ollantay,* discovered in 1816 among a number of manuscripts belonging to Father Antonio Valdez, but most likely presented for the first time in the presence of rebel leader Túpac Amaru in Tinta, near Cuzco, the same year he led the most extensive of several Indian rebellions: 1780. The play is based on the legend of Ollantay, who rebels against King Inca Pachacútec for not being allowed to marry into the nobility. Now considered a true expression of Quechua literature before the conquest, there is some agreement that the play was probably never formally preserved on the set of knotted strings used to keep track of things, never maintained in its original form through oral tradition, and not considered an omen of future ethnic rebellions. It is seen as a combination of an indigenous theme and Spanish colonial dramatic form, perhaps one of the first transitional texts combining the Old and the New World's literary forms.

Except in isolated rural areas, much indigenous literary expression in the form of religious prayer, drama, and spectacle—including myth, legend, fable, poetic expression of human feelings, and ritual song—was lost during the colonial period. With the creation of San Marcos University in Lima in 1551 and the arrival of the printing press, literature in Quechua was quickly suppressed by the Spanish crown. Also noteworthy is the simultaneous importation of popular literary forms from Spain, such as ballads, proverbs, folksongs, and lyric or narrative poems that documented contemporary historical events and personal folly with satire—events such as civil war and illicit love affairs among Spaniards in the New World. In fact, the *romance,* a long-winded form of narrative poetry, accompanied the conquistadors to Peru and served as a vehicle for anonymous soldiers to later evoke actual events they witnessed as new territories were conquered. As mentioned, colonial literature, then, begins to thrive on two opposing forms in Spanish, one of which is erudite, formal, institutional, and written, while the other is popular, spontaneous, and oral. Somewhere in between fall the early chronicles that recorded and recounted in semiofficial fashion the discovery-conquest and its fateful aftermath. The first chroniclers were men such as Francisco Pizarro's secretaries, Francisco de Jerez and Pedro Sancho de la Hoz, who participated in the sixteenth-century military campaign and included personal observations of the Peruvian land and people in *Verdadera relación de la conquista del Perú* (The True History of the Conquest of Peru;

1634) and *La relación para su Majestad* (A History for His Majesty; written in 1534, published in Italian in 1556), respectively. Both works portray Pizarro and the conquistadors in a positive light in order to justify their violent exploits to the king. A form of chronicle writing in Peru, offering a more carefully rendered, impartial, general history of the period, is *Crónica del Perú* (Chronicle of Peru), written by Pedro Cieza de León (1519–1554?). The first part was published in Seville in 1553, while other parts remained unpublished until recent times.

Opposite views, found in indigenous testimony recorded in other chronicles of the time of conquest, are also important in order to understand both sides of the conflicts of that age. One such testimony is Felipe Guamán Poma de Ayala's (1535?–1615?) *La nueva corónica y buen gobierno* (First New Chronicle and Good Government), completed in 1615. Guamán Poma de Ayala's manuscript somehow made its way to Europe and was not discovered until 1908 in the Royal Library of Copenhagen. Written to Spanish King Phillip II as a defense of the Andean people, the document is almost 1,200 pages in length and contains some 400 drawings that depict the New World inhabitants living under Spanish rule. Guamán Poma de Ayala's treatise represents not only a strong invective, accompanied by pictures, against the Spanish conquerors, but is also an appeal to rectify their iniquities. Finally, it is worth noting that since the discovery of Guamán Poma de Ayala's text, his apparently incorrect use of Spanish has been widely discussed and criticized. Today, linguists are studying the relationship between Quechua and Spanish in order to show how uncommon usage in Spanish can be attributed to the underlying influence of grammatical and lexical structures in Quechua. No real Spanish models existed for the writer, and historical reality had pitted two different linguistic structures—and, in fact, verbal and visual icons representing European and New World cultures—against each other.

Other chroniclers, that is, the indigenous and mestizo writers, occupy an important position in the literary history of colonial Peru, setting the stage for creative symbiotic relationships in art and culture from that time forward. The giant among this group of writers is Inca Garcilaso de la Vega (1539–1616). His literary fame is based primarily on his *Comentarios reales de los Incas* (Royal Commentaries of the Incas; volume I, 1609; volume II, 1617). The *Comentarios* were published in two parts, the first in Lisbon in 1609 and the second, entitled *Historia general del Perú* (General History of Peru), in 1619 in Córdoba, where Garcilaso de la Vega is buried. Born of Inca and Spanish parents in Cuzco where he grew up, Inca Garcilaso de la Vega left for Spain in 1560, never to return to his native land. Unable to obtain compensation in Spain for his father's participation in the conquest in Peru, he became a captain in the Spanish army and participated in quelling a

Inca Garcilaso de la Vega.

Moorish uprising in the Alpujarras, a southern mountain range. Leaving the service, he turned to educating himself after reading the Renaissance historians and literary giants, having begun to compile information for his definitive work, *Comentarios reales*, four years earlier.

Understandably somewhat idealized, the first part of the *Comentarios* is interesting for its documentation of Inca civilization from its beginnings, including its government, folklore, customs, and legends. The second part details historical events following the conquest and has been considered an attempt to justify Spanish actions in Peru. Inca Garcilaso de la Vega has been criticized for an apparently anti-Indian stance in his work, but he was also adept at presenting a positive image of the Incas while providing a clear picture of European cruelty, believing the Incas were destroyed before they were ever understood. What makes the *Comentarios* stand out from other texts of the time is their literary nature, on the one hand, and the ideological significance of the project on the other. His study of Renaissance texts allowed him a much freer use of imagination in his writing about history, but the work was also conceived as a profound search for personal and collective identity. Its self-reflective, autobiographical nature provides a vehicle for the modern reader to understand Garcilaso de la Vega's struggle to give some sense and order to a tumultuous historical moment in the world. For these reasons, the *Comentarios* is considered to be the starting point for a long line of great mestizo writers from Peru.

The transition from the early chronicle and somewhat later historical treatise—not to mention the standard religious documents that came off the first printing press in Peru—to fictionalized narrative, poetry, and theater came quickly during the colonial period. One of the first texts that sought to combine fact and fiction is *El lazarillo de ciegos caminantes* (The Guide for Blind Wayfarers; 1776), written by Alonso Carrió de la Vandera (1715–1783). The mestizo protagonist, who engages in dialogue with the author, uses the alias Concolorcorvo to recount his trip as a postal inspector from Buenos Aires to Lima in 1771. Several contemporary styles and elements—picaresque narrative, travelogue, literary sketches, jokes, swear words, and Inca folklore—are fused to create humor, satire, and irony critical of the Spanish colonial empire. A travelogue secretly published in Lima, the book is an interesting account of the long trip and provides information about many aspects of colonial life: transportation routes, cost of living, food supplies and production, and the dangers of isolated travel. The work is critical of inefficient government administration, and, since the author was himself a government bureaucrat, he cloaks the identity of the narrator in fictitious characters who do the work of creating the document. While some believe the work is essentially a piece of literature, it does provide information about the peoples Concolorcorvo met along the way, their customs and habits, and their flora and fauna. The text by Concolorcorvo is a transitional piece moving toward greater awareness of the growing problems of colonial government that would eventually lead to its downfall.

## Poetry

Poetry written in the classical mode for the court and family of the viceroy by Spanish and Peruvian poets flourished between 1550 and 1630. Diego de Hojeda (1572?–1615), one of many poets born in Spain but who went to Peru at an early age, wrote the important poem "La Cristiada" (The Passion of Christ; Seville, 1611), which draws upon classical and religious traditions to retell the Passion of Christ in twelve epic-style cantos. *La Cristiada* was written around the time a woman writing under the pen name "Amarilis" sent her poetry to Lope de Vega, one of Spain's most famed poets of the Golden Age period, who then published it with a response in *La Filomena* (1621). Another poet was an anonymous woman who wrote a poem in tercets entitled "Discurso en Loor de la Poesía" (A Discourse in Praise of Poetry), a Neoplatonic philosophical, yet highly sensual, poem that appeared as a prologue in Diego Mexía de Fernangil's *El Parnaso Antártico* (Antarctic Poetry; Seville, 1608). One of the most important poets of that epoch was Juan del Valle y Caviedes (1650?–1697), who wrote much in the style of Francisco de Quevedo's *Conceptismo* (a Baroque style stressing the use of wit and conceits). Caviedes produced hundreds of poems and several theatrical pieces, which carried his trademark of irony, satire, and biting social criticism. Caviedes's principal poetic work, *Diente del Parnaso* (The Tooth of Parnassus), which was written in 1689 but not published until 1873, consists of dozens of poems that not only poke fun at Peruvian society in general, but also expose and condemn the medical profession for its lack of ethical standards.

## Drama

Drama also played a major role in colonial literature, especially the short pieces aimed at a creole audience that was reflected in their structures and thematic content. Caviedes wrote three plays in Lima in the seventeenth century: *Entremés del amor alcalde* (The Mayor's Love), *Baile del amor médico* (The Dance of the Doctor's Love), and *Baile del amor tahur* (The Dance of the Trickster's Love), all of which are parallel in structure, consisting of several interlocutors and a protagonist who answers questions. The works compare love to jail, sickness, and gambling. In 1719, Pedro de Peralta y Barnuevo wrote *La Rodoguna* (A Comedy: Rodogune), a mythological comedy based on *Rodogune*, by the French seventeenth-century playwright Corneille, in which a father discovers his daughters, Mariquita, Chepita, Panchita, and Chanita, in compromising situations with their respective tutors. Peralta y Barnuevo wrote other short pieces as well, and he is also known for his epic play *Lima fundada* (Lima Founded; 1732).

## THE END OF THE EMPIRE: THE LATE EIGHTEENTH CENTURY AND EARLY NINETEENTH CENTURY

Serious economic, social, and political problems—dwindling mineral and agricultural production, hunger, misery, exploitation, stagnating commercial profits resulting from an asphyxiating state monopoly, and burdensome taxation—culminated at the end of the eighteenth century, leading to outright physical rebellion and overt written protest as seen, respectively, in the 1780 Túpac Amaru rebellion, the critical writings of a new generation of liberal intellectuals, spontaneous poems that circulated anonymously among the masses, and the new ideas espoused in numerous political speeches in Lima. Among the most famous is *Elogio* (Eulogy; 1771), delivered valiantly by José Baquíjano y Carrillo (1751–1818) in the halls of San Marcos University and directed against the tyranny of the newly arrived viceroy. Reformist attitudes became widespread as seen in the writings of Juan Pablo Viscardo y Guzmán (1747–1798), whose *Carta a los españoles americanos* (Letter to the Spanish-Americans) is now considered the first declaration of independence. In 1792, the seminal newspaper *Mercurio Peruano* (The Peruvian Mercury) began publication, expounding ideas of the Enlightenment and dealing with contemporary themes such as the social function of the intellectual, climatic and sociological studies, the importance of a general language in Peru, and the importance of higher education. While it was not an organ of liberation, the *Mercurio Peruano* created a space for intellectual change and growth in Peru.

By 1814, popular poetry inciting the masses to revolution could be heard openly on the streets. Popular poetry and song praised liberty, affirmed the notion of independence, and attempted to recover Peru's indigenous past by highlighting local customs. Written expressions of incipient Romantic tendencies—independence, nationalism, freedom of expression, and individualism—are seen in the works of Mariano Melgar (1790–1815). Melgar is considered one of the few mestizo poets to lay the groundwork for the birth of an authentic Peruvian poetry. His works include the revival of certain pre-Columbian themes (feelings of abandonment and solitude, and the transformation of older love songs and poetry) into Andean poetic musical compositions known as *yaravíes*. This renovation of ancient native poetic forms marked a major step toward literary emancipation in Peru.

Under the leadership of Simón Bolívar, Spanish colonial rule was dealt its death blow in South America when the colonial forces were finally defeated at the battle of Ayacucho, Peru, in 1824. Yet, in Lima, several centuries of colonial splendor and aristocratic frivolity had bolstered conservative thinking enough that, soon after independence, Peruvian intellectual forces found themselves drawing other types of battle lines in an attempt to build a national literature. One such was between European universalist schools of thought (supported by those who, belonging to aristocratic families, distrusted the new republican government) and national-regional nativist tendencies (found mainly in Lima's middle-class writers). The former group was identified with the writings, mainly sketches depicting local color, called *Costumbrismo* published in *El espejo de mi tierra.* (The Mirror of My Land; 1840) by Felipe Pardo y Aliaga (1806–1868). Other writers, such as Manuel Ascensio Segura (1805–1871), also typify local color sketches and went on to write about the growing dissatisfied urban bourgeoisie in Lima. Asencio Segura's best known play, *Ña Catita* (Ms. Catita; 1856), is a comedy about a married couple who are always fighting, and their latest conflict is over their daughter's two suitors. Ña Catita is the figure who gives conflicting advice to the parents and stirs up trouble between them. Today, the majority of these writers are considered to be "colonialized writers" because of their nostalgic look backward to colonial times and their conservative viewpoints regarding sociopolitical change. The opposition between the universalists and regionalists induced writers at the time to give serious attention to the function of art as a form of responsibility to society.

## A New Phase: The Late Nineteenth Century and Early Twentieth Century

Peruvian literature reached a crossroads at end of the nineteenth century in the works of two important writers, Ricardo Palma (1833–1919) and Manuel González Prada (1844–1918). Palma was a liberal Romantic writer who became famous for creating a type of narrative called the *tradición*, consisting of numerous volumes of local color sketches that span from 1863 to 1915, and spawning many imitators throughout Spanish-speaking America. González Prada is known for his literary essays, *Pájinas libres* (Free Pages; 1894) and *Horas de lucha* (Time to Fight; 1908). Palma's literary genre, a hybrid form of the short story, brought together history and literary invention through popular stories, chronicles, legends, myths, and proverbs to capture with irony and humor the days of the aristocratic, popular, but mainly creole life at the seat of the Peruvian viceroyalty in the colonial period. Hence, Palma is responsible for creating a mythical arcadian "City of the Kings," a stereotypical image of the Spanish dream that did little more than mask a more problematical reality. Nevertheless, Palma's writing represents an interesting combination of historical and literary discourse, and his *tradiciones* are exemplary forms of writing that attempt to create a distinct national literature in Peru.

Questioning Palma's nostalgic desire to return to a colonial aristocratic society, González Prada seized the moment to look forward and rebuild national conscience through his essays. By 1886, he had established the Literary Circle (Círculo Literario) to promote new ideas. González Prada's famous essay *Discurso en el Politeama* (Discourse in the Politeama; 1888) signals insurrection on the literary establishment by younger intellectuals and writers. His pronouncement, "Send the old to the grave and the young to work!" ran counter to Palma's ideas on national reconstruction, and it split intellectuals into two camps on issues such as the function of literature in society. González Prada became famous for questioning everyday in Peruvian society. Palma and González Prada vehemently attacked each other over many issues, one of which was the value of the Spanish legacy when defining a modern nation. In time, González Prada radicalized his thinking about the dominance of Spanish culture in Peru to the point that he saw himself as a socialist. His essays and oratory were the vehicles by which he was able to analyze issues such as how a national literature should function as a tool for conscience-raising and the importance of creating a literary space enabling other marginalized voices to have a place in the literary canon.

During this period, other intellectuals came to the forefront, fomenting cultural awareness in Peru. Of singular importance is Clorinda Matto de Turner (1852–1909), whose ideas on socially committed literature marked the beginnings of new literary perspectives. Matto de Turner participated actively in literary groups in Cuzco and Lima. Her fame rests mainly on her realist-naturalist novel *Aves sin nido* (Birds Without a Nest; 1889), which exposes the plight of downtrodden Indians in society. *Aves sin nido* is her most widely read novel in contemporary times. Its theme concerns the exploitation of indigenous groups that are enslaved to religious and economic institutions. In the novel, characters recognize the need for change and wonder how to bring it about. Also writing novels at this time from the perspective of progressive realism was Mercedes Cabello de Carbonera (1845–1909), whose principal work, *Blanca Sol* (White Sun; 1889), underscores the moral bankruptcy in contemporary Peruvian society by re-creating the superficial and trivial life of a woman determined to get what she wants by any means available to her. She fails, is shunned by society, and becomes a lesson for the reader.

## MODERNISM IN PERU

While the impact of Spanish-American Modernism was being felt elsewhere through the poetry of the Nicaraguan Rubén Darío, this literary movement was not strongly cultivated in Peru. The narrative *Cuentos malévolos* (Malevolent Stories; 1904) by Peru's Clemente Palma (1872–1946) falls under the Modernist rubric. Ricardo Palma's son wrote within the conventional model of the nineteenth-century short story established by Poe and developed turn-of-the-century themes of catastrophe and despair.

Peruvian turn-of-the-century writers and intellectuals, namely José de la Riva Agüero (1885–1944), Francisco García Calderón (1883–1953), Ventura García Calderón (1886–1959), and Víctor Andrés Belaúnde (1883–1966), wrote about the country's long past and its relationship to the future from a position of refined elegance and conservative idealism. While de la Riva Agüero wrote essays stressing the importance of understanding European culture and bolstering university scholarship, Ventura García Calderón re-created local environments, regional dialects, and peculiar customs in his collection of short stories *La venganza del cóndor* (The Revenge of the Condor; 1924), his characters facing universal themes of cruelty, injustice, and misfortune. Belaúnde published essays such as *Peruanidad* (On Being Peruvian; 1903) and *El Perú moderno y los modernos sociólogos* (Modern Peru and Modern Sociologists; 1908), using a historical-sociological perspective to portray Peruvian identity.

A Modernist poet who became singularly famous beyond Peru's borders was José Santos Chocano (1875–1934). He was a liberal activist in both literature and politics who published many volumes of emotionally combative poetry. Santos Chocano's *Alma América* (The Soul of America; 1906), subtitled *Poemas indo-españoles* (Indian-Spanish Poems), is his most famous work. With an epiclike tone, the poet recounts Peru's history and describes its geography, flora and fauna, and human cultures. His verses carried "the majesty of the Inca and the pride of the Spaniard." A world traveler, Santos Chocano became known as "The Poet of America" (El Poeta de América) during his lifetime.

Writing poetry at the same time was José María Eguren (1874–1942), a Modernist whose work went beyond Modernist aesthetics and brought Peruvian poetry into the twentieth century. Eguren created imaginary worlds in which he found seclusion. Steeped in French Symbolism, his poetry dwells on certain motifs such as mystery, love, and dreams. His three books of poetry—*Simbólicas* (Symbolisms; 1911), *La canción de las figuras* (The Dance of the Figures; 1916), and *Poesías* (Poems; 1929)—are lyrical, symbolic, and imaginative. They enrich the Spanish language with regional words, archaic terms, neologisms, and even foreign and invented words. His works also lead Peruvian poetry into the twentieth century because themes of alienation, skepticism, doubt, and lack of creativity are the driving forces behind a poetry that takes the reader into the esoteric spheres of the imagination and the spiritual world, suggesting the arrival of the Avant-garde movement.

## THE AVANT-GARDE PERIOD: THE 1920S AND 1930S

The Avant-garde period of the 1920s in Peru witnessed a surge of experimentation in poetry and the appearance of many literary journals that served as organs for the diffusion of new ideas from Europe. Noteworthy poets include Carlos Oquendo de Amat (1905–1936), César Moro (1903–1956), Martín Adán (1908–1985), and Emilio Adolfo Westphalen (1911–2001). But the literary giant who transformed not only Peruvian but all Latin American poetry was César Vallejo (1892–1938). Vallejo was from a small provincial town in the northern Andes mountains and is famous for his books of poetry that include *Los heraldos negros* (The Black Heralds; 1919), *Trilce* (1922), *Poemas humanos* (Human Poems; 1939), and *España, aparta de mí este cáliz* (Spain, Let This Cup Pass from Me; 1939). Vallejo's poetic voice speaks of pain, suffering, and existential isolation in his search for identity in the modern world. His first book projects a feeling of doubt about the world as it looks backward nostalgically to family and home in the mountains in a search for universal feelings of love and caring. His second book, *Trilce*, rocked the literary world in Peru by treating certain themes—the destruction of a felicitous past, love, incarceration, modern absurdity, the search for meaning—with unconventional strategies, such as experimentation with ellipses, typographical arrangements, conceptual wordplay through antithesis, repetition, colloquialisms, archaic terms, and neologisms. Coming full circle from the expression of existential doubt in the first book and accepting the lack of any identifiable substance in contemporary absurdism in his second, Vallejo, in his third book, sought unity and solidarity with a proletarian audience of anonymous citizens through which love becomes an answer to the world's problems and forms the basis for a new collective human social order. Tensions abound in all three books, from dialectical forces in the first books to collective integration and salvation in the third book. A poet of the Avant-garde era, Vallejo's poetry represents the poetic process itself within a historical framework. Vallejo transformed language and, in the process, changed reality. In 1923, Vallejo left Peru forever and traveled to Paris, where he died in 1938 at the age of forty-four.

## JOSÉ CARLOS MARIÁTEGUI AND THE INDIGENIST MOVEMENT

On a broader scale, a major intellectual figure in Peru was José Carlos Mariátegui (1894–1930). Mariátegui founded *Amauta* (1926–1930), one of the most important journals in Latin America, and organized the Socialist Party of Peru. His essays probe the ideological nature of Peruvian society from a Marxist perspective. He sought to stimulate political, social, ethnic, and economic reforms in Peru by objectifying problems through incorporating scientific, historical, and sociological perspectives in his writing: "Create a new Peru within a new order." Mariátegui's concerns nurtured the debate about the question of mestizo society in Latin America, leading to the famed Indigenist Movement in Peruvian art and literature. The Indigenist Movement gave way to a broader approach that sought to broach the totality of American ethnic reality, the product of which is mestizo culture, considered by Mariátegui the truly authentic expression of all societies of the New World.

In 1941, Indigenist Regionalism as a literary movement in Peru took a significant turn. At that time, Ciro Alegría (1909–1967) reached a new artistic level in his writing career with *El mundo es ancho y ajeno* (Broad and Alien Is the World; 1941), and José María Arguedas (1911–1969) produced his first novel, *Yawar fiesta* (1941). Indigenism here refers to a writing process in which author, text, and reader are not from the ethnic group being described in the novel. The process begins in the nineteenth century with Indianism, a variant of fiction writing that portrays the Indian as the typical "noble savage" from a European perspective. The second variant—Indigenism—is seen early on in works by Clorinda Matto de Turner, mainly because her writing communicates an awareness of deep-rooted social problems and takes a position of social protest. Even though her novel *Aves sin nido* is basically anticlerical, and the indigenous characters are portrayed in romantic fashion, the exploitation of Indians is forcefully condemned. During the Indigenism phase, stronger communicative ties are forged between the indigenous world in the Andes and the rest of the country, particularly the urban white or mestizo social groups on the coast. Mariátegui's Marxist ideology also contributed to a deeper understanding of the social, political, and economic problems facing indigenous groups in Peru.

Ciro Alegría, the son of a prominent landowner in northern Peru whose property included Indian peons, is particularly well-known for three important novels: *La serpiente de oro* (The Golden Serpent; 1935), *Los perros hambrientos* (The Hungry Dogs; 1939), and *El mundo es ancho y ajeno*, the latter of which was translated into English and won the coveted Farrar and Rinehart prize in the 1940s. The latter narrates the expulsion of an indigenous community from its lands in the northern Peruvian Andes and communicates a strong sense of injustice against the Indians. The novel has a noticeable earth-tied regionalist quality about it, for it also describes the symbiotic relationship between the Indians and their sacred lands. The text is quite diffuse in terms of theme and structure. The basic story line is replete with numerous digressions that describe the problem of coca addiction, the presence of the looming jungle region to the east, the exploitive work on the coast, stories about several characters' pasts, ideas on social relationships among Peruvians, as well as segments that present communal stories, myths, songs, and super-stitions. In fact, the community's demise is foreshadowed at the book's be-ginning when a snake crosses the path of Rosendo Maqui, the community leader who curses his bad luck as he fails to catch the snake and mutilate it with his machete. The narrative process moves in different directions: from a feeling of unity among the group to the dispersion of the community's members; from a straightforward, linear narration to an intentionally scat-tered series of scenes, stories, and character biographies; from characterization based on interior monologue to exaggerated stereotypes and romantic figures in society; and from a sense of hope to one of complete gloom and the feeling of loss and pessimism when, at the end, the young and progressive future leader of the community, Benito Castro, is killed as army troops move in to expel the Indians from their lands. Alegría's fiction acquires an epic tone and yet maintains a human quality about it.

José María Arguedas incorporated into his work his firsthand experiences as a child among Quechua-speaking Indians in southern Peru and as a ded-icated, anthropologically trained researcher of culture and cultural conflict. Born in the Andes, Arguedas's father was white and his mother Indian. He studied anthropology in Lima and later taught Quechua and ethnology at San Marcos University before committing suicide in 1969. Whereas Alegría constructed his worlds around general themes, such as humans against nature and Western civilization against indigenous culture, in his books *Agua* (Wa-ter) and *Yawar fiesta* Arguedas examines infinitely more complex worlds of opposition and conflict from decidedly cultural perspectives. His ever-widening narrative process begins by examining not just conflict between whites and Indians, but also between Indians and mestizo landowners. He then proceeds to examine regional cultural conflicts between populations living in the Andes and those living on the coast. By uncovering serious problems in each stage and communicating a strong defense of the Indians, Andean culture, and the Peruvian nation respectively, Arguedas's progression demonstrates the need to be aware of the exploitation of the Indians by mestizos, and the domination over the inhabitants of the Andes by coastal society and culture.

*Los ríos profundos* (Deep Rivers; 1958) is undoubtedly Arguedas's most popular novel. It narrates the rites of passage of fourteen-year-old Ernesto, whose early years were spent living in an Indian community and who now finds himself experiencing culture shock in a provincial town, where he en-counters exploitation of ethnic cultures (Indians) by the dominant religious, political, and economic forces in a highly stratified and fragmented society. The protagonist narrates a series of incidents while at a boarding school run by priests. From his dual cultural heritage, Ernesto inherits sensitivity and emotion, empowering him to live within a world of magic and myth, while at the same time perceiving and describing both in minute detail and symbolically serious social problems. The important episode in the novel involving the uprising of the women who work in the town market is a fine example of social protest. Repeatedly, common objects take on magical qualities and provide a way of understanding the delicate relationship between human beings and their world. The Inca walls of Cuzco become dynamic, living forces that recall the city's glorious past; the rivers possess certain magical powers that help Ernesto understand his environment; and the small spinning top that he plays with is a vehicle making musical sounds that carry Ernesto back in time and connect him with his cultural past. The novel's success lies in a subtle combination of varied reader experiences: universal themes such as the young protagonist's coming of age, the effect of realist, detailed description of his environment and memorable characters, a critical look at the effects of ethnic discrimination, and the symbolism of common objects that take on magical qualities and provide understanding of the protagonist's past and present. This combination of elements catapults Arguedas's works beyond conventional indigenist writing to a level that incorporates the indigenous world of Peru into a larger realm.

Meanwhile, efforts to stem the tide of pessimism and apocalypse in Peru can be found in the continuing proclivity for indigenist writing, particularly in the narrative works of Manuel Scorza (1928–1984). Scorza's political leanings led him to write about the problems of Peru's Indian communities from the perspective of a politically committed unionizer, bringing modernity and justice to the rural areas. Highly readable for their storytelling component, criticism of injustice in the highlands, and strong doses of "magical realism," Scorza's five-volume series of novels, called ballads (*baladas*) or songs (*cantares*), narrate not only the persistent drive of an Indian community to regain its lands and legal rights, but also the utopian hope that once again outside assistance, this time based on union consciousness and the magical collaboration of sympathetic animals and nature, will solve the Indians' problems. Scorza's novels are a curious mixture of myth-and-legend-brought-to-life and testimony of historical fact based in part on a rebellion of the Yanacocha community in the department of Cerro de Pasco (1959–1962), in which Scorza participated, and the massacre of many of those involved. After he denounced the participation of the Peruvian military in the carnage, he was forced to flee to France, where for the next ten years he wrote many works, the most important of which are *Redoble por Rancas* (The Toll of the Bells for Rancas; 1977), *Cantar de Agapito Robles* (The Song of Agapito Robles; 1977), and *La danza inmóvil* (The Stationary Dance; 1983).

## THE 1950S AND 1960S

As in other Latin American countries, novelists, short story writers, and literary essayists in Peru have always been the nation's true sociologists, narrating the lives of the heretofore silenced voices of disenfranchised classes of Indians, mestizos, and blacks, as well as the urban lower class and the bourgeoisie. These writers, born in the 1920s and 1930s, began to document the enormous socioeconomic changes that were taking place, not only in the rural provinces, but also in the growing cities beginning in the 1950s. Such is the case of Sebastián Salazar Bondy (1924–1965), Julio Ramón Ribeyro (1929–1994), Oswaldo Reynoso (1932), and Enrique Congrains (1932), who focused their attention on the problems facing the urban proletariat living in shantytowns, and other marginalized bourgeois living on the economic and social fringes of society. Meanwhile, other writers continued to develop themes that dealt with conflicts of power, culture, and society in the provinces and rural areas of Peru, involving not so much the Indians of Arguedas's novels, but more the coastal and inland mestizos and cholos (Indians) as they were confronted with a growing influence of modern culture from the coast. Eleodoro Vargas Vicuña's *Nahuín* (1953) and *Taita Cristo* (Father Christ; 1963), and Carlos E. Zavaleta's *El Cristo Villenas* (Christ Villenas; 1955) and *Los Ingar* (The Ingars; 1955) are texts that deal with provincial city and rural village conflicts of cultural values tied to religion, superstition, political organization, and impinging economic forces.

When Salazar Bondy published his essay *Lima la horrible* (Lima the Horrible) in 1964, he portrayed the demise of a national project to create a new urban Peru, centered mainly in Lima. The essay chastises the *limeño* (natives of Lima) for continuing to pretend to live in the make-believe world of the colonial period that apparently signifies power and wealth, but is now out of step with the decaying, anachronistic world of an overgrown urban environment.

Among the writers of this period who have been mentioned so far, the one who stands out, beginning in the 1950s, for his engaging stories and novels is Julio Ramón Ribeyro. Ribeyro lived in Paris in the early 1950s but returned to Peru in the 1990s shortly before his death in 1994. During that time, he produced three novels, *Crónica de San Gabriel* (Chronicle of San Gabriel; 1960), *Los geniecillos dominicales* (The Sunday Rascals; 1965), and *Cambio de guardia* (Change of Guard; 1976), and several short story collections, reprinted in the four-volume *La palabra del mudo* (The Word of a Mute; 1972–1992). In addition, Ribeyro published plays that were all included in *Teatro* (Theater; 1975), literary essays in *La caza sutil* (The Subtle Hunt; 1976), a three-volume diary, *La tentación del fracaso* (The Temptation of Failure; 1993–1995), *Prosas apátridas* (Prose Without a Nation; 1975), and *Dichos de Lúder* (Luder's Sayings; 1989). Among his early short story collections, two volumes are notable: *Los gallinazos sin plumas* (Vultures Without Feathers; 1955), his first, and *Tres historias sublevantes* (Three Subversive Stories; 1964). The former treat the problems of the proletariat in Lima, such as the story that gives the title to the collection. It focuses on the exploitation of young children who are forced to sift through garbage to earn a living for their abusive grandfather. Other stories delve into the petty, superficial nature of the urban bourgeois. The latter collection presents socioeconomic problems of Peruvians living in three distinct regions: the coast, the Andes, and the Amazon jungle region. These stories are excellent examples of regional transcendentalism, taking the reader away from local environments to levels of universal condemnation of injustice. The success of Ribeyro's stories is based on their varied themes and narratives of typical situations of Peruvian everyday life. Ribeyro's stories are built around coincidence, fate, insanity, confusion of identity, moral values, mediocrity, and, of course, the dismal living conditions affecting marginal members of society.

## THE MILITARY ERA AND THE LATE 1960S

Completing the panorama of well-known, Peruvian fiction writers are Mario Vargas Llosa (1936) and Alfredo Bryce Echenique (1939). Both have numerous literary works to their credit and continue to write and receive international recognition. Their vast repertoire of writings not only include novels and short stories but also literary criticism and journalism. Vargas Llosa's novelistic trajectory spans more than thirty years. His first novel, *La ciudad y los perros* (The Time of the Hero; 1963), was the first Latin American novel to be published by the prestigious publishing house Seix Barral in Barcelona, and set the stage for the appearance of the so-called Boom writers of the 1960s: Gabriel García Márquez, Julio Cortázar, Carlos Fuentes, and José Donoso. Preceded by a collection of short stories entitled *Los jefes* (The Bosses; 1958), Vargas Llosa's first novel, along with *La casa verde* (The Green House; 1966) and *Conversación en La Catedral* (Conversation in the Cathedral; 1969), represent his initial Neorealist phase of writing. This trilogy of sorts attempts to create tightly structured yet panoramic mosaics of Peru's people and its problems, by creating a microcosm of Peruvian society, by using a real military school in Lima as a backdrop for drama and social commentary in *La ciudad y los perros*, or by juxtaposing and intertwining plots that simultaneously develop different locations (the jungle and a northern desert city in *La casa verde*).

Through midcentury and continuing into the 1960s, a notable spirit of

Novelist Mario Vargas Llosa. Courtesy of *World Literature Today.*

progressive thinking, frank dedication to sociopolitical change, and the creation of the cultural foundation of modernity among young people who grew up in that era were squelched by repressive governments, something that quickly led to a feeling of bitter failure and deep anxiety in a whole generation of artists and writers. In fact, moving beyond the polarizing effects of certain conventional oppositions—urban and rural environments, ethnic differences between whites and Indians, geographical differences between the Andes mountains and the coastal region—significant novels by several Peruvian fiction writers probe the effects of the eight-year dictatorship (1948–1956) of Manuel A. Odría, which has been characterized as having stunted the intellectual growth of an entire generation by blocking, through censorship and political corruption, the social mechanisms for creating contemporary culture in Peru. Novels such as *Los geniecillos dominicales* by Julio Ramón Ribeyro, *Conversación en La Catedral* by Mario Vargas Llosa, and *Un mundo para Julius* (A World for Julius; 1970) by Alfredo Bryce Echenique, are loosely structured around the initiation process of young people who suffer from the destruction of conventional social structures and who question the possibility of integrating themselves into contemporary Peruvian reality, in which dictatorship has sapped the moral strength of society through corruption, theft, blackmail, assassination, and sexual taboo.

The characters in these novels suffer from anxiety, pessimism, loss of spiritual values, apathy, and solitude. Vargas Llosa's *Conversación en La Catedral* re-creates a world of frustration and failure on multiple levels of Peruvian society through some seventy characters who move across urban and rural landscapes of poverty and wealth, exploitation and abuse, power and alienation. However, one character, Santiago Zavala, is developed more fully; the novel follows approximately twelve years of his life between the ages of eighteen and thirty, a period that corresponds historically to 1951–1963. Santiago, a journalist, communicates a feeling of malaise and pessimism throughout the novel.

## THE 1970S AND BEYOND

Alfredo Bryce Echenique's first novel, *Un mundo para Julius*, is a charming, well-written piece of literature; it is about a youngster's first years of life, until he reaches eleven. However, adult and child perspectives intermingle to create poignant irony, great humor, and penetrating social commentary about the relatively uncomplicated, rich, upper-class strata of Peruvian society in Lima in the 1950s. To date, Bryce Echenique has written four volumes of short stories and eight other novels: *Tantas veces Pedro* (So Many Times Pedro; 1977), *La vida exagerada de Martín Romaña* (The Exaggerated Life of Martín Romaña; 1981), *El hombre que hablaba de Octavia de Cádiz* (The Man Who Talked about Octavia de Cádiz; 1985), *La última mudanza de Felipe Carrillo* (Felipe Carrillo's Last Move; 1988), *Dos señoras conversan* (Two Ladies Chat; 1990), *No me esperen en abril* (Don't Wait for Me in April; 1995), *Reo de nocturnidad* (Prisoner of Night; 1997), and *La amigdalitis de Tarzán* (Tarzan's Tonsillitis; 1998).

The writing of *Un mundo para Julius* and its subsequent publication in 1970 coincided with the 1968 coup d'état that expropriated vast land holdings from Peru's oligarchy. Not surprisingly, literature and history fused to symbolize the destruction of Peru's old ruling classes, making Bryce Echenique's book very much a novel of its time. It won the 1972 Peruvian National Prize for Literature and continues to generate interest for contemporary readers. The novel is not only an engagingly corrosive portrayal of the pretentious, morally blind Peruvian oligarchy and its transition to the dominant nouveau-riche class, subsidized by an influx of North American capitalism in the 1950s, but also an early postmodern urban novel in which the bildungsroman structure and its questioning, sentimental protagonist Julius brings together the the drama of lost innocence, a black comedy of manners, playful parody, and social satire.

It is not surprising that the development of political themes in contemporary Peruvian fiction became more intense in the 1970s. The previous twenty-five years in Peruvian history were ones of successive military coups d'état, and it is probably not a coincidence that several fiction writers produced novels dealing with the military and dictatorship. While Vargas Llosa's *Conversación en La Catedral* represents the novel of disaffected youth during the 1950s under military dictatorship, it also opens the door to a series of novels published between 1970 and 1976, novels that scrutinize and, ultimately, collectively condemn the dominance of the military in Peruvian society. Those works include *Las rayas del tigre* (The Stripes of the Tiger; 1973) by Guillermo Thorndike, *La ronda de los generales* (The Turn of the Next General; 1973) by José B. Adolph, *Pantaleón y las visitadoras* (Captain Pantoja and the Special Service; 1973) by Mario Vargas Llosa, and *Cambio de guardia* by Julio Ramón Ribeyro.

Vargas Llosa continued his long-standing feud with machismo and military "bossism" (*caudillismo*) in *Pantaleón y visitadoras*. In contrast to the seriousness of his earlier works, Vargas Llosa used humor to turn the concept of militarism into a mockery of itself. To accomplish this he created a seemingly absurd story in which the military sends Captain Pantoja to the jungle region of Peru to organize a flotilla of prostitutes to service sex-starved soldiers assigned to isolated military posts. The absurd plot, that is the Captain's manic drive for organization, the irony coming out of the humorous situations, and the grotesque nature of certain events in the novel go far in condemning not only the military but also different variants of fanaticism in society.

Finally, in *Cambio de guardia* Julio Ramón Ribeyro shares with the reader an innovative view of Peruvian politics by presenting a collective vision of multiple characters in Peruvian society in the throes of a coup. The novel focuses on the far-reaching yet little discussed effects of the covert politicking that normally accompanies this type of political change. Moral indignation, disgust, and condemnation of military coups are typical reader responses to Ribeyro's novel. In one sense, these political novels look at society from the perspective of numerous characters who form a faceless mass of marginalized people, portraying the unfortunate effects of military dictatorships on society at large. Yet, these novels also possess a particular perspective and language that serve to create a more subjective vision based on a particular character; as a result the reader can feel the effects of corrupt politics on the lives of all the characters.

After Vargas Llosa's 1977 novel *La tía Julia y el escribidor* (Aunt Julia and the Scriptwriter), which deviates from his original social neorealist stance of the 1960s toward comedy in a serious spoof on the act of writing, he has gone on to produce additional astounding works of fiction. *La guerra del fin del mundo* (The War of the End of the World; 1981), a voluminous tome similar to his earlier works for its depiction of violence, brutality, and human chaos, is a challenging response to these charges. This novel re-creates a historical incident that serves to underscore the author's thematic obsession with ideological fanaticism. It deals with events at the turn of the century in the impoverished backlands of northeastern Brazil, near Canudos, where a massacre of thousands of religious fanatics by the Brazilian army took place. Basically, the novel's retelling of the incident communicates the idea that certain religious phenomena might be more important than historical influences in determining human conduct. The truth of Canudos is found less in its historical documentation than in the myths and superstitions that still live today.

The intensification of political violence in Peru beginning in the early 1960s is documented in Vargas Llosa's next novel, *Historia de Mayta* (The Real Life of Alejandro Mayta; 1984), which narrates the attempts of a Peruvian novelist to reconstruct a failed leftist uprising in the Andes mountains led by an old schoolmate, Alejandro Mayta. The story revolves around interviews that a novelist-turned-reporter conducts with family and acquaintances in order to create Mayta's chaotic vision of the world. Together, Vargas Llosa's last three novels—*¿Quién mató a Palomino Molero?* (Who Killed Palomino Molero?; 1986), *El hablador* (The Storyteller; 1987), *Elogio de la madrastra* (In Praise of the Stepmother; 1988)—represent the rich narrative diversity that has become his trademark. The first novel captures in melodramatic fashion the secret passions of men and women that make for good storytelling. Relying on those narrative techniques of detective fiction that create ambiguity, yet stress the conviction that reality and truth are indeed illusions, Vargas Llosa plays with the reader's curiosity from the outset by posing a question in the title that is never satisfactorily answered. The second novel narrates the story of a university student, Saúl Zuratas, who drops out of society and joins an Amazon jungle tribe to become a storyteller. The collision between civilization and so-called primitive tribes is at stake, and the novel asks the question whether it is possible to integrate different cultures into modern society, or whether isolated Indian tribes should be preserved. *Elogio de la madrastra* (In Praise of the Stepmother; 1990) ventures into the realm of erotic literature, in which perversity and pleasure are experienced through the perspective and detailed descriptions of a character who revels in hedonism and the clever intertextual juxtaposition of narrations by figures that appear in paintings by the great masters of Western tradition.

Vargas Llosa's literary production suffered a hiatus shortly after the publication of *Elogio de la madrastra* as he entered the Peruvian political arena, losing the presidential race to President Alberto Fujimori in 1990. An account of his political defeat is his memoir, *El pez en el agua* (A Fish in the Water; 1993). Also from 1993 is *Lituma en los Andes* (Death in the Andes), a novel set in the Peruvian highlands that can be read as a remake of the Greek myth of Dionysus transposed to the Andes. As Lituma, the protagonist, tries to shed light on missing members of the community of Naccos, he discovers the confrontation between local myths in the Andean collective psyche and rational Western thought. Vargas Llosa returns at length to the characters of *Elogio de la madrastra* in *Los cuadernos de Don Rigoberto* (The Notebooks of Don Rigoberto; 1998), an erotic divertimento that did not receive the critical acclaim of his previous novels. However, Vargas Llosa's mastery as a novelist would be proven once again in his latest book, *La fiesta del chivo* (The Feast of the Goat; 2000), a riveting and violent portrayal of General Rafael Leonidas Trujillo's dictatorship in the Dominican Republic between 1930 and 1961.

Vargas Llosa's international stature has not eclipsed other contemporary Peruvian writers. Bryce Echenique, for instance, as well as many others, have created their own narrative worlds alongside Vargas Llosa's looming corpus. Other significant contemporary narrative texts pick up on the earlier theme of disaffected youth in a modern, morally corrupt Peruvian society, as well as themes of societal violence, class and racial exploitation, and loss of ethnic identity: *A la hora del tiempo* (When Time Beckons; 1977) by José Antonio Bravo (1937– ), *El viejo saurio se retira* (The Ancient Lizard Retires; 1969) and *La violencia del tiempo* (The Violence of Time; 1991) by Miguel Gutiérrez (1940– ), and *La vida a plazos de don Jacobo Lerner* (The Fragmented Life of Don Jacobo Lerner, 1978) by Isaac Goldemberg (1945– ). The diversity of narrative themes in contemporary Peruvian literature reflects the variety of cultural representations in Peru, making the affirmation of a "standard" national Peruvian literature difficult. Goldemberg narrates the historical past of a Jewish immigrant to Peru and his own efforts to preserve and even affirm his identity. In a similar vein, *Canto de sirena* (The Siren's Song; 1977), and *Crónica de músicos y diablos* (Chronicle of Musicians and Devils; 1990) by Gregorio Martínez (1942–   ) create a new panorama of heretofore unknown voices in literature, Peru's black population.

Peruvian narrative in the 1980s and 1990s developed around four general tendencies:

1. A subjective personal perspective that focuses more on the development of individual characters and captures the feeling of skepticism and implicit negativity of individuals, rather than on facing social and historical concerns that have led to alienation and nonconformity. Examples include Alonso Cueto's (1954–   ) *La batalla del pasado* (The Battle of the Past; 1983), *Deseo de noche* (Evening Desire; 1993), and *Demonio del mediodía* (Noon Demon; 1999); *Caballos de medianoche* (Horses on the Midnight Range; 1985) and *Una mujer no hace un verano* (One Woman Does Not Bring Summer; 1995) by Guillermo Niño de Guzmán (1955–   ); *No se lo digas a nadie* (Don't Tell Anyone; 1994), and *La noche es virgen* (The Night Is Virgin; 1997) by Jaime Bayly (1965–   ); *Caramelo verde* (Green Candy; 1992) by Fernando Ampuero (1949–   ); *Al final de la calle* (Dead End Street; 1993) by Oscar Malca (1968–   ); and *Canon perpetuo* (Perpetual Canon; 1993) and *Salón de belleza* (Beauty Salon; 1994) by Mario Bellatín (1960–   ). In all of these examples, realism gives way to an exploration of individual obsessions.

2. The reconstruction of history through the incorporation of official documents and oral narratives that not only bring to life past events, but also reinterpret them in modern terms, as in *Yo me perdono* (I Forgive Myself; 1998) by Fietta Jarque, and *Sol de los soles* (Sun of the Suns; 1998) by Luis Enrique Tord.

3. The presentation of Peruvian reality in a crude and direct fashion that attempts to capture in an epic mode the daily travails of everyday, almost carnivalesque, urban and rural poverty, seen in works such as *Patíbulo para un caballo* (Firing Squad for a Horse; 1989) by Cromwell Jara (1951–   ).

4. Portraits of the Peruvian Amazon as in César Calvo's (1940–   ) *Las tres mitades de Ino Moxo y otros brujos de la Amazonía* (The Three Halves of Ino Moxo and Other Medicine Men of the Amazon Jungle; 1981); and neoindigenous perspectives in *País de Jauja* (Country of Jauja; 1993) and *Libro del amor y de las profecías* (The Book of Love and Prophecy; 1999) by Edgardo Rivera Martínez (1933–   ) and *Ximena de dos caminos* (Ximena at the Crossroads; 1994) by Laura Riesco (1940–   ).

5.  The presence of novels and short stories by women, such as *Las dos caras
    del deseo* (The Two Faces of Desire; 1994) by Carmen Ollé (1947–  ),
    *La mujer alada* (The Magic Woman; 1994) by Viviana Mellet
    (1959–  ), *Ojos que no ven* (Eyes That Don't See; 1998) and *Me envol-
    verán las sombras* (Shadows Will Surround Me; 1998) by Leyla Bartet;
    and *Ave de noche* (Evening Bird; 1996) and *Puñales escondidos* (Hidden
    Knives; 1998) by Pilar Dughi (1956–  ), among others. Recent Peruvian
    narrative does not purport to impose current political ideologies or rein-
    terpret history, but rather to pose more questions than provide answers
    to the urgent social problems that have beset the country in recent dec-
    ades.

## POETRY

Peruvian poetry after World War II became polarized after a debate in the
1950s between the social-realists and the so-called purists. Writing at the
time was a group of poets born in the 1920s: Javier Sologuren (1922–  ),
Alejandro Romualdo (1926–  ), Jorge Eduardo Eielson (1924–  ), Washington Delgado (1927–  ), Carlos Germán Belli (1927–  ), Juan Gonzalo
Rose (1928–1983), and Blanca Varela (1926–  ). Sologuren began publishing purist poetry, that is, lyrical, balanced, architecturally structured poetry
in the 1940s in collections such as *El morador* (The Boarder; 1946) and
*Detenimientos* (Detainments; 1948), and he continued to publish regularly
through the 1960s, 1970s, 1980s, and 1990s. He published *Vida contínua:
obra poética* (Continuing Life: Poetic Works) in 1989. In a realist vein, Romualdo's *Edición extraordinaria* (Extraordinary Edition; 1958) communicates a concern for social issues and problems affecting Peruvians from a
conceptual perspective of ideas that seek to portray the human condition as
determined by politics. Delgado discovered early on an endearing personal
poetic formula that looks at love, nostalgia, and social commitment in unique
ways. He has published over a half-dozen books since the 1950s, winning
the Premio Nacional de Poesía (National Poetry Prize) in 1953. *Un mundo
dividido. Poesía, 1951–1970* (A Divided World. Poetry, 1951–1970; 1970)
is a collection of poems that covers twenty years of writing.

Blanca Varela, one among many Peruvian woman poets, began publishing
poetry in 1959 with a collection entitled *Ese puerto existe* (That Port Exists;
1959). Other significant books by Varela include *Canto villano* (Village Song;
1978), *Ejercicios materiales* (Material Exercises; 1993), and *El libro de barro*
(The Book of Clay; 1993). Often introspective, her poetry seeks to probe
everyday events to find significant realities that provide new perspectives on
life. A modern parallel to Vallejo's creative syntax, neologisms, and daring

imagery is Carlos Germán Belli's poetry. He astutely combines different types of language—scientific, archaic, slang—as well as distortion and black humor to produce sarcastic perspectives that capture the failure and frustration of urban dwellers in contemporary society who are alienated from each other, their history, and their culture. His most important books of poetry include *¡O hada cibernética!* (Oh Cibernetic Muse!; 1961), *El pie sobre el cuello* (The Foot on the Throat; 1964), *En alabanza del bolo alimenticio* (In Commemoration of Unchewed Food; 1979), *Más que señora humana* (More Than a Humane Señora; 1986), *En el restante tiempo terrenal* (The Rest of Worldly Time; 1988), *Trechos del itinerario* (Moments of the Itinerary; 1998), and *En las hospitalarias estrofas* (Hospitable Verses; 1998).

The generation of 1960, a loosely defined group of younger poets born in the 1940s, is characterized by similar concerns for contemporary humanity. It includes Rodolfo Hinostroza (1941– ), Antonio Cisneros (1942– ), Javier Heraud (1942–1962), Marcos Martos (1942– ), Julio Ortega (1942– ), Mirko Lauer (1947– ), Luis Hernández (1941–1977), and Ricardo Silva-Santisteban (1941– ). The group has become a significant generation linking the great poets of the past (Vallejo, Eguren, and Adán) to the urgent need for change experienced by the more recent poets of the 1960s. The common denominator among these younger poets seem to be change. The concept became the driving force for the construction of new theories and ideas. Cuba, rampant urbanization and industrialization, radical political developments, and the premature death of Javier Heraud, the poet-turned-guerrilla killed by government forces in the jungle town of Puerto Maldonado, triggered the need to formulate new attitudes and the desire not only to alter but also to reaffirm certain important values in society. Heraud's poetry, published in *El río* (The River; 1960) and *El viaje* (The Trip; 1961), revolves around themes involving social commitment, revolution, loneliness, love, and death. Exploring an ever-widening panorama of new realities, this group of poets develops themes concerning Peruvian history, social criticism such as alienation in contemporary society, and traditional values such as family and intimate relationships.

Without a doubt, Antonio Cisneros (1942– ) is the most well-known contemporary poet. His poetry includes such important works as *Destierro* (Banished; 1961); *David* (1962); *Comentarios reales* (Royal Commentaries; 1964), which won the Premio Nacional de Poesía in 1965; *Canto ceremonial contra un oso hormiguero* (Ceremonial Song Against an Anteater), which received the Cuban Casa de las Américas prize in 1968; *Agua que no has de beber* (Water That's Not For Drinking; 1972); *Como higuera en un campo de golf* (Like a Figtree on a Golf Course; 1972); *El libro de Dios y de los húngaros* (The Book of God and the Hungarians; 1978); *Crónica del Niño*

*Jesús de Chilca* (Chronicle of the Baby Jesus of Chilca; 1981); *Monólogo de la casta Susana y otros poemas* (Monologue of the Chaste Susana and Other Poems; 1986); and *Las inmensas preguntas celestes* (The Immense Blue Questions; 1992).

Peruvian poetry in the 1980s and 1990s is marked by a feeling of deception, bitterness, and exploration of the self. Two decades of chaos and violence destroyed youthful enterprise and vigor. Also, the election of a conservative, rightist party in 1980 and the sudden domination of the Shining Path guerrilla movement led Peru toward destruction in the 1990s. As a result, the relationship between poetry and society has become complex, due to a process of dispersion that has hindered the creation of literary groupings or solidarity movements that formed in earlier periods. Such is the case of the poetry of many poets born between the 1940s and 1960s and who publish since the 1970s: *Primera muchacha* (First Girl; 1997) by Jorge Pimentel (1944); *El guardián del hielo* (The Guardian of Ice; 2000) by José Watanabe (1946); *El mundo en una gota de rocío* (The World in a Drop of Mist; 2000) by Abelardo Sánchez León (1947); *Angelus Novus* (Angelus Novus; 1989) by Enrique Verástegui (1950); *Aquí descansa nadie* (No One Rests Here; 1998) by Carlos López Degregori (1952); *Violencia de sol* (Violent Rays; 1980); and *Altagracia* (Highest Pardon; 1989) by Enrique Sánchez Hernani (1953); *Y si después de tantas palabras* (And If After so Many Words; 1992) by Sandro Chiri (1958); *Archivo de huellas digitales* (Archive of Finger Prints; 1985); and *Naufragio de los días* (Shipwrecked Days; 1999) by Eduardo Chirinos (1960); *La ceremonia del adiós* (The Farewell Ceremony; 1997) by Giovanna Pollarolo (1952); and *Mariposa negra* (Black Butterfly; 1994) by Rocío Silva Santisteban (1963).

In the twentieth century there was an unprecedented wealth and variety in Peruvian letters; now writers face the challenge of incorporating new voices into the literary canon as history evolves and new issues of cultural identity and representation are debated.

## REFERENCES

Adorno, Rolena. *Guaman Poma: Writing and Resistance in Colonial Peru*. Austin: University of Texas Press, 2000.

Adorno, Rolena, Mercedes López-Baralt, Tom Cummins, John V. Murra, Teresa Gisbert, and Maarten van der Guchte. *Guamán Poma de Ayala: The Colonial Art of an Andean Author*. New York: Americas Society, 1992.

Aldrich, Earl M. *The Modern Short Story in Peru*. Madison: University of Wisconsin Press, 1966.

Ferreira, César, and Ismael P. Márquez, eds. *Los mundos de Alfredo Bryce Echenique*

*(Textos críticos)*. Lima: Fondo Editorial Pontificia Universidad Católica del Perú, 1994.

Foster, David William. *Peruvian Literature: A Bibliography of Secondary Sources*. Westport, CT: Greenwood Press, 1981.

Gerdes, Dick. *Mario Vargas Llosa*. Boston: Twayne Publishers, 1985.

González Vigil, Ricardo, ed. *Antología de la poesía peruana Siglo XX, vols. I–II*. Lima: Petroperú, 1999.

———. *El cuento peruano* 1975–1979. Lima: Petroperú, 1983.

———. *El cuento peruano* 1980–1989. Lima: Petroperú, 1997.

———. *El cuento peruano* 1990–2000. Lima: Petroperú, 2001.

Higgins, James. *A History of Peruvian Literature*. Liverpool, England: Francis Cairns Publications, 1987.

———. *The Poet in Peru*. Liverpool, England: Francis Cairns Publications, 1982.

Kohut, Karl, José Morales Saravia, and Sonia V. Rose, eds. *Literatura peruana hoy: Crisis y creación*. Frankfurt-Madrid: Vervuert, 1998.

Kristal, Efraín. *The Andes Viewed from the City: Literary and Political Discourse on the Indian in Peru, 1848–1930*. New York: Peter Lang, 1987.

———. *Temptation of the Word: The Novels of Mario Vargas Llosa*. Nashville, TN: Vanderbilt University Press, 1998.

Márquez, Ismael P., and César Ferreira, eds. *Asedios a Julio Ramón Ribeyro*. Lima: Fondo Editorial Pontificia Universidad Católica del Perú, 1996.

Ortega, Julio. *Crítica de la identidad: La pregunta por el Perú en su literatura*. Mexico City: Fondo de Cultura Económica, 1988.

Ossio, Juan. "Myth and History: The Seventeenth-Century Chronicle of Guamán Poma de Ayala." *Text and Context: The Social Anthrolopology of Tradition*. Ravindra Jain, ed. Philadelphia: Institute for the Study of Human Issues, 1977: 51–93.

Poma de Ayala, Guamán. *Nueva corónica y buen gobierno*. Franklin Pease G.Y., ed. 3 vols. Lima: Fondo de Cultura Económica, 1993.

Vega, Garcilaso de la. *Royal Commentary of the Incas and General History of Peru*. Austin: University of Texas Press, 1966.

Vilanova, Núria. *Social Change and Literature in Peru (1970–1990)*. Lewiston, NY: The Edwin Mellen Press, 1999.

Wood, David. *The Fictions of Alfredo Bryce Echenique*. London: King's College London Hispanic Series, 2000.

# 6

# Performing Arts and Cinema

## CINEMA

### The Silent Era

THE HISTORY OF Peruvian cinema began in 1897 with rudimentary projections of silent films. When compared to other parts of the world, Peruvian cinema was a relative latecomer.

European film was already booming when the first samples of Peruvian cinema appeared, portraying primarily scenes of daily life. This period in cinema history also witnessed the birth of feature films. Peruvian cinema did not easily adapt to the new trend of long-playing films, but some silent feature films did eventually appear.

The birth of Peruvian film was greeted by a very restricted upper-crust audience in tune with developments in France. In the wake of the world economic crisis of 1929, which affected the Peruvian economy, ticket sales witnessed a dramatic decline. Unfortunately, these circumstances combined with the unreliable technology available to Peruvian filmmakers, had a direct impact on film production, and few advances were made during this period.

### Talkies, the 1930s, and Amauta Films

Sound arrived in Peru on November 29, 1929, with the premiere of Edward H. Griffith's *Capitán Calaverón* (Captain Skull and Bones) at Lima's Colón Theatre. Even though the film contained audio portions, there was no dialogue. The growing public demand for talkies led movie houses to acquire the technology necessary for these films, and, as a result, Peruvian audiences were able to see the great Hollywood productions of the 1930s.

The first Peruvian film containing sound, Alberto Santana's *Resaca* (Hangover), premiered in 1934. Others soon followed including *Cosas de la vida* (The Facts of Life; 1934) and *Buscando olvido* (Trying to Forget; 1936). Sound represented a break with the traditional imagery of the silent era and movie screens became inundated with scenes from domestic existence and daily life. In fact, sound and dialogue defied the mere reliance on dramatic gestures that had characterized silent films. Now, able to identify with the speech and accents of the characters on the screen, Peruvian audiences embraced talking films, and cinema emerged as an indispensable source of social and anthropological information.

Production of feature-length films in Peru began in 1937, due in large part to the efforts of Manuel Trullen, a Spaniard; Alberto Santana, a Chilean; and Francisco Diumenjo, an Argentine. That same year witnessed the birth of Amauta Films, a production company founded with the backing of Felipe Valera La Rosa, a Peruvian businessman. Trullen and Diumenjo were also involved with the company, which eventually produced fourteen films and 100 documentaries and newsreels by 1940. That year, Amauta Films relinquished its role in moviemaking to concentrate on film distribution. Nevertheless, Amauta Film's endeavor represents the first attempt to produce films that were Peruvian in both content and production. The use of sound allowed audiences to identify with the characters and situations in the films, and the dialogue echoed their own experiences. An important film director of this period was Sigifredo Salas, who made a number of popular films including *Gallo de mi galpón* (The Rooster in my Shed; 1938), *El guapo del pueblo* (The Good-looking Man of the People; 1938), *Palomillas del Rímac* (The Scoundrels of Rimac; 1938), and *Tierra linda* (Beautiful Land; 1939), among others.

Amauta produced mainly comedies and melodramas with characters drawn from the middle and lower classes. An attempt was made to recapture the essence of realist folkloric drama, with its language and environment, since this type of setting and dialogue was already very popular among Peruvian audiences. It was not unusual for film actors to appear on the stage or even be involved in radio. However, as the 1940s dawned, the city of Lima was changing and the stereotyped characters traditionally favored by Peruvian filmmakers were now giving way to an emergent urban working class. Amauta stubbornly refused to take heed of the changing times and continued to idealize in its films a vision of society that no longer had any basis in reality.

Amauta Films released its last film in 1940. The shortage of raw materials caused by World War II, the expansion and success of the Mexican film industry, and Amauta's own lack of access to the latest film technology all contributed to the closing of its production company.

## The 1940s

In 1940, National Films of Peru was formed under the auspices of Felipe Valera La Rosa. That same year the company released its first film, Kurt Hermann's *Alerta en la frontera* (Border Alarm). 1945 brought *La Lunareja*, directed by Bernardo Roca Rey. A subsequent string of box-office flops forced National Films to close in 1947. The production company Huascarán was founded at about the same time, but it also failed miserably. The unfortunate demise of these two companies left a vacuum in the production of Peruvian films that would last about ten years. However, foreign films, especially Mexican, enjoyed great success during that time.

In hindsight, the most important event pertaining to the film industry would be the establishment in 1940 of the first legal guidelines for the regulation of film production and screening by President Manuel Prado. The encouragement of Peruvian-made documentaries and newsreels on a wide range of subjects was the stated goal of his decree. All movie houses in the country were required to show them before their feature presentations. These guidelines would remain in effect until 1954.

## The 1950s

The 1950s were a fruitful time for the production of feature films in Peruvian cinema. The film industry managed to stay afloat by producing documentaries and short films with cultural content. The School of Cuzco (*Escuela Cuzqueña*), led by the brothers Manuel and Víctor Chambi, both sons of one of Peru's most famed photographers, Martín Chambi, made a significant contribution to Peruvian filmmaking, making the Andean world and its people the focus of their productions. Moreover, they increased public interest in the cinema through the establishment of the Cuzco Film Club (*Cine Club del Cuzco*).

Unlike film production, film distribution had enormous success. Viable distribution companies were formed and numerous movie houses opened their doors for the first time. This was the golden age of Mexican cinema and also of the great Hollywood films, both eagerly received by Lima's movie-going public.

### The 1960s

The arrival of television in 1958 heralded the expansion and growing acceptance of a new form of mass media entertainment. The audience's favorite characters were those appearing in soap operas and other television programs, and film companies took advantage of this popularity by giving the same actors starring roles in feature films. One example of this trend is the Peruvian film *Nemesio* (1969), in which Tulio Loza plays a character he made famous on television; another is Kiko Ledgard's *El embajador y yo* (The Ambassador and I), released in 1968. Although hits at the box office, neither film should be considered a critical success. Other contemporary films were *Tres vidas* (Three Lives; 1967), directed by Aquiles Córdova; *Interpol llamando a Lima* (Interpol Calling Lima; 1969), directed by Orlando Pessina; and *Milagro en la selva* (Miracle in the Jungle; 1965) and *Boba diabólica* (Nefarious Fool; 1968), both directed by Enrique Torres Tudela.

Interest in the Andes as a subject matter produced important films such as *Kukuli* (1961), codirected by Eulogio Nishiyama, Luis Figueroa, and César Villanueva; and *Jarawi* (1966), codirected by Nishiyama and Figueroa.

Also noteworthy during this decade was the publication of *Hablemos de cine* in 1965, the first movie journal to establish professional film criticism in Peru. Founded by the journalist Isaac León Frías, there were seventy-seven issues of *Hablemos de cine*, an unprecedented number by Latin American standards. It included among its contributors some of the most well-known critics and film directors in contemporary Peruvian cinema: Reynaldo Ledgard Federico de Cárdenas, Francisco Lombardi, Ricardo Bedoya, José Carlos Huayhuaca, and Augusto Tamayo San Román, among others.

### The 1970s

In 1972, the military government led by Juan Velasco Alvarado promulgated Decree No. 19327, known as the Law for the Development of the Film and Cinematographic Industry. Its provisions required movie houses to show something with Peruvian content before the presentation of any foreign film. This state of affairs chiefly benefited the makers of short films, who supplied theaters with the Peruvian-made movies they desperately needed in order to comply with the decree. The growth in domestic production gave young experimental filmmakers a creative outlet, and also afforded them the opportunity to hone their skills in the practical techniques of moviemaking. However, while a large number of these Peruvian films were made in the 1970s, most are notable only for their lack of originality and an acute absence of fine craftsmanship, both in terms of technique and style.

## The 1980s

Peru's economic plight during the 1980s dramatically affected its film industry. Producers wanted an immediate return on their investment before inflation could eat away revenues and, at the same time, drive up interest rates on the loans all filmmakers needed in order to survive. Faced with this difficult situation, producers resorted to imaginative and cheap techniques, such as video and low-cost story lines rooted in popular humor and satire. Several films reflect this trend, including *Los siete pecados cardenales y mucho más* (The Seven Deadly Sins and a Whole Lot More; 1985), directed by Claudio Barrios; *Los Shapis y el mundo de los pobres* (The Shapis on the Other Side of the Tracks; 1986), directed by Juan Carlos Torrico; *Fantasías* (Daydreams; 1987), directed by Efraín Aguilar; and *El Rey* (The King; 1987), also directed by Juan Carlos Torrico.

The goal of producers was to capture as much as possible of Peruvian everyday life on film. Their works contained a lively critique of social reality in which Peruvians weather a cutthroat society wracked by social and political upheaval with humor and incisive wit. *La fuga del chacal* (The Escape of the Jackal; 1987), directed by Augusto Tamayo San Román, and *Profesión: detective* (Profession: Criminal Investigator; 1986), directed by Juan Carlos Huayhuaca, are the most notable examples of this school of Peruvian filmmaking.

The 1980s also saw Luis Llosa direct *Misión en los Andes* (Mission in the Andes; 1987) and *Calles peligrosas* (Mean Streets; 1989), films more concerned with exposing audiences to an imaginary future that had little in common with the everyday problems faced by Peruvians. Llosa would later direct several action films released in the United States, including *Sniper* (1993), *The Specialist* (1994), and *Anaconda* (1997). Other film directors of note who still remain active in Peru include Alberto Durant, Marianne Eyde, Luis Felipe Degregori, Edgardo Guerra, Federico García, and Aldo Salvini.

## Armando Robles Godoy and Francisco Lombardi

Two film directors who have left a mark on Peru's contemporary film history are Armando Robles Godoy (1923–  ) and Francisco Lombardi (1942–  ).

Robles Godoy first appeared on the Peruvian film scene in the 1960s. A film enthusiast and critic for the daily *La Prensa*, he was the first director to realize that the art of filmmaking requires more than technical mastery: above all else, movie directors must forge an expressive language that bonds filmgoers with the characters on the screen. During the 1960s, Robles Godoy was a great admirer of European cinema, especially of innovative existentialist directors such as Resnais, Antonioni, and others. These directors wanted to help the audience discover and define the film's meaning on their own, so that it would have relevance to their own experience.

In 1965, Robles Godoy released *Ganarás el pan* (You'll Get Your Bread) and a year later, *En la selva no hay estrellas* (In the Jungle You Can't See Any Stars). Although these films were somewhat low-key in terms of their ex-pressiveness, they differed greatly from films of other Peruvian directors of Robles Godoy's generation, illustrating the director's intention of exploring the hidden individual struggles of his characters. Whereas traditional Peru-vian movies had been characterized by shoddy production values and hack-neyed scriptwriting, Robles Godoy demanded a high level of technical finesse in his art. Discarding the unoriginal and forgettable story lines prevalent in mainstream cinema, he relied on tightly woven plots to explore the psycho-logical depth of his characters. His films tried to present multiple viewpoints and sensations to the audience by means of a superbly crafted contextual framework, innovative combinations of time and space, and painstaking ed-iting. Such is the case with Robles Godoy's most internationally acclaimed film, *La muralla verde* (The Green Wall), which premiered in 1970. It tells the story of a young couple who move from Lima to the Peruvian jungle in the hope of making a living as farmers on a small piece of land near the town of Tingo María. Tragedy strikes, however, when their young son is bitten by a snake and dies. The film is partially based on Robles Godoy's real life experiences. As a youth, the director moved to the jungle and tried to break down the "green wall" of the jungle.

Most noteworthy in *La muralla verde* is Robles Godoy's original filming technique, presenting his viewers with the lush setting of the jungle and people's intention to prevail in this environment. Robles Godoy uses flash-backs and intermingles them with the thoughts of his characters in the pres-ent to develop the family tragedy. At other times, close-ups and zoom shots capture the dark threats of the powerful world that surrounds the characters. The rambling structure is not only necessary to provide background and explain the action of the film, but also to illustrate people's struggle with the dark forces of nature that will ultimately defeat them.

In 1973, Robles Godoy released *Espejismo* (Optical Illusion). In the 1980s, he directed the Cinematographic Workshop (Taller de cinematografía) in Lima, and released *Sonata soledad* (Lonely Sonata; 1987). Despite the few titles to his credit in feature films, the latest of which is *Imposible amor* (Impossible Love; 2000), Robles Godoy's influence and originality as an artist and filmmaker are unquestionable. He remains an active participant in Peru's cultural scene and continues to produce documentaries and features for television.

Francisco Lombardi is Peru's most acclaimed film director at the present time. His accomplishments include twelve feature films, several of which have received important awards at major international film festivals. Most of his movies depict the many social tensions that lie beneath the surface in contemporary Peruvian society. Lombardi's earlier films include *Muerte al amanecer* (Death at Dawn; 1977), *La muerte de un magnate* (Death of a Tycoon; 1980), and *Maruja en el infierno* (Maruja in Hell; 1983). However, it was *La cuidad y los perros* (The City and the Dogs; 1985) that brought international attention to Lombardi's work. Based on the novel *The Time of the Hero* (1963) by Mario Vargas Llosa, Peru's most important contemporary novelist, it tells the story of a young man's upbringing in Lima's Leoncio Prado military academy and his eventual disillusionment with the military structures, the corrupt power they represent, and the violent system they enforce. Violence and social struggle are at the center of *La boca del lobo* (The Lion's Den; 1988), one of Lombardi's most celebrated films, which was nominated for an Academy Award for best foreign film. *La boca del lobo* is a riveting film that narrates the bloody clash between the Peruvian army and the guerilla group Shining Path in a small Andean village in the 1980s.

The 1990s proved to be Lombardi's most prolific decade yet. He released the highly successful *Caídos del cielo* (Fallen from the Sky; 1990), a grim black comedy set in the inflation-ridden Lima of the 1980s. By intertwining three different stories from three different social classes, the film offers a metaphorical rendering of the crises affecting Peruvian society at that time. Lombardi later directed *Sin compasión* (Without Compassion; 1994), an adaptation of Fyodor Dostoyevsky's novel *Crime and Punishment*, and *Bajo la piel* (Under the Skin; 1996). In 1998, Lombardi released *No se lo digas a nadie* (Don't Tell Anyone), based on the novel by author and journalist Jaime Bayly. A controversial film, it reveals the downward spiral of a young man, Joaquín, searching for his sexual identity. Joaquín's domineering father and religious mother offer no alternative for him but to find his own way in life. Upon entering college, he meets new friends outside of his privileged social circle, and, while coming to terms with his gay identity, he plunges into a life of drugs, sex, and violence. Ultimately, he befriends Alejandra, who could save him from self-destruction, but, instead, Joaquín chooses to run away. The rigid, intolerant moral code of Peru's conservative upper class is well depicted in this film, and, as in many of Lombardi's films, his protagonist is faced with a crucial personal dilemma that will leave a scar on his personal identity.

Lombardi's next film was *Pantaleón y las visitadoras* (Captain Pantoja and the Special Service; 1999). Based on yet another novel by Mario Vargas Llosa, it tells the hilarious adventures of an army captain entrusted with the task of clandestinely organizing a prostitution service for the sex-starved troops stationed in the Peruvian jungle. The movie is as much a poignant satire of a loyal and disciplined officer as a well-crafted caricature of the Peruvian military as an institution. Lombardi's latest opus is *Tinta roja* (Red Ink; 2000), a scathing exposé of yellow journalism in Latin America, based on a novel by the Chilean writer Alberto Fuguet.

Lombardi's by now long and artistically mature movie career remains a milestone in the difficult history of film in Peru. While commercially successful, more importantly his movies represent an artistically mature and insightful portrayal of the many issues surrounding contemporary Peruvian society.

## THEATER

In his book *Actores de Altura: Ensayos sobre el teatro popular andino* (Actors of the Highlands: Essays on Andean Popular Theater; 1992), anthropologist Luis Millones sheds light on the many types of performance activities that took place in Peru before the arrival of the Spaniards, pointing out the importance that such activity took on after the bloody conquest. Millones quotes from the sentence to death by torture of Túpac Amaru II, an Indian leader who rebelled against Spanish authorities in Cuzco in the 1780s. Referring to Inca dramatic events, the magistrate of Cuzco, José Antonio Areche, who issued the death sentence of Túpac Amaru, specifies: "That they are not to be performed in any of the towns within the province or in any other public events customarily used by the natives to commemorate their ancient Incas." Millones then refers to writers such as Guamán Poma de Ayala, Santa Cruz Pachacuti, and the Inca Garcilaso de la Vega to evoke theatrical events used by the Inca for ideological and administrative purposes in agricultural rituals and for civic and military celebrations. Moreover, it is a well-established fact that theater developed even before the political domination of the Inca empire in the coastal ceremonial centers, from the thousand-year-old expansion of the Chavín culture in the central Andes, to the Nazca, Moche, and Chimú cultures on the coast of Peru, as control of water and soil became increasingly more regulated into a more complex economic and social integration. The arrival of the Spaniards and the bloody persecution of pagan gods never succeeded in eliminating dramatic expression or the use of theater as a means of ideological resistance among the indigenous population.

### The Colonial Period

Just as theater was used as a medium of ideological indoctrination during the time of the Inca, it also served as an instrument of Christian indoctrination among the Indians by Spanish missionaries during the colonial period. However, its main cultivators were not Spaniards but natives assimilated into the new social and political order. In his lengthy history of Peruvian literature, Augusto Tamayo Vargas links Inca theater to colonial theater using two very concrete examples: the multitudinous event that the Inca Pachacútec ordered to celebrate the triumphant return from Quito of his son Túpac Yupanqui, and the course followed by the play *Ollantay*, written in Quechua and later translated into several languages, and questioned for its European structure and temperament. Tamayo mentions other plays, which, like *Ollantay*, were also performed in Quechua during colonial times: *El hijo pródigo* (The Prodigal Son), written in the seventeenth century by the Cuzco playwright Juan Espinosa Medrano, nicknamed *El Lunarejo*; *El pobre más rico* (Rich Man Poor Man), written in the seventeenth century by Gabriel Centeno de Osma; and *Usca Páucar*, the work of an unidentified eighteenth-century author. While these plays mantain certain features of pre-Columbian drama and indigenous features such as the use of a chorus and traditional Quechua images, they can also be linked to the tradition of Spanish Golden Age theater. In fact, amidst the violent environment of the conquest and attracted by the artistic wealth of Golden Age drama, it is a well-known fact that Spaniards in the Americas made theater their preferred form of entertainment, along with bullfighting, Indian-hunting with fierce dogs, and cockfights.

As early as 1563, Spanish Golden Age drama was performed in Lima with plays by Lope de Vega, Calderón de la Barca, and Tirso de Molina. Spectators filled church porticos as much as they did the playhouses and palace halls. At the same time, the Jesuits wisely resorted to theater to indoctrinate the indigenous population, even manipulating Inca theater with native actors. In 1670, Lima hailed *El gran teatro del mundo* (The Great Theater of the World) by Calderón de la Barca, having been moved the previous year by the premier of *Rosa de Lima*, which celebrated the beatification of Saint Rose of Lima during the government of the Count of Lemos, one of the most influential supporters of theater productions during the colonial period.

### The Republican Period

The war for independence was not fertile ground for the development of theater. One of the most representative characters of the first years of the

Republic appeared was the popular Niño Goyito (Master Goyito), the protagonist of *Un viaje* (A Voyage; 1840), by Felipe Pardo y Aliaga (1806–1868), and *Las tres viudas* (The Three Widows; 1862), *El Sargento Canuto* (Sargeant Canuto; 1839), and *Ña Catita* (Ms. Catita; 1856), by Manuel Ascensio Segura (1805–1871). In honor of these playwrights, two theaters in Lima bear their names. Apparently, the humor of the literature of manners, also known as *costumbrismo*, could not stop to reflect on major historical events. Moreover, during the second half of the nineteenth century, *costumbrismo* buried reflective theater, given that in the midst of Spanish *zarzuelas* (operettas) and comedies, no major playwright emerged. However, many visiting theater companies kept the interest alive among the public and when in the 1930s theatrical changes began, the public was there to support the genre. During this time, actors and producers such as Leonardo Arrieta, Lucho Córdova and Roger Retes are names to be remembered in the rebirth of theater.

The late 1930s and 1940s saw a rebirth in Peruvian theater. Various institutions helped establish a national theater and bring it in line with international trends. In 1938, the Asociación de Artistas Aficionados (Association of Amateur Artists), popularly known as the AAA, was founded, as well as the Teatro de la Universidad de San Marcos (Theater of San Marcos University) in 1941. Similarly, the Actors Union was founded in 1945, and the Escuela Nacional de Arte Escénico (National School of Scenic Art, ENAE) in 1946, which forged the first generation of trained actors: Luis Alvarez, Manuel Delorio, Nilda Núñez, and Jorge Montoro, among others. The ENAE would later produce two of Peru's most internationally reknowned actors in the 1960s: Saby Kamalich and Ricardo Blume. Thanks to government support, National Theater Awards were granted for the first time in 1946 to Juan Ríos for *Don Quijote* and to Percy Gibson Parra for *Esa luna que empieza* (That Beginning Moon). The following year, Sebastián Salazar Bondy's *Amor, gran laberinto* (Love, a Great Labyrinth) was staged. These plays marked a renewal of Peruvian theater, breaking with the *costumbrista* tradition in favor of a nonmimetic representation of local reality and a concern with more universal themes.

Another important event during this time was the arrival of Spain's Margarita Xirgú Company to perform a number of plays by Federico García Lorca. Xirgú's artistic excellence and fame proved decisive for the growth of contemporary Peruvian theater. Edmundo Barbero and Santiago Ontañón, two members of the company, stayed on in Lima at the end of the season. Soon after, Barbero was appointed director of the ENAE and Ontañón went on to train generations of set designers, including his best disciple, Alberto Terry. Terry was an active scenographer in many important plays until he became part of the television industry in the late 1950s.

The 1950s saw an increase in theatrical activity with the staging of many foreign plays by touring companies, the emergence of new drama groups, and the publication of important works by Peruvian playwrights. In 1956, the López Lagar Company staged Strindberg's *Father*, helping to fire up the already restless theatrical environment, so diversified that the Gassols Brothers Children's Company could alternate their musical comedies with classical pieces directed by Ricardo Roca Rey in the porticos of the Cathedral of Lima and the Cathedral of San Francisco, supported by a growing AAA. This variety called for playwrights, such as Juan Ríos, Sebastián Salazar Bondy, Enrique Solari Swayne, Felipe Buendía, and groups with innovative theatrical ideas, such as the Club de Teatro de Lima (Lima Theater Club) in 1953, and Histrión, Teatro de Arte (Histrionic Art Theater) in 1957. Such talent soon gave rise to the Teatro Nacional and the opening of La Cabaña theater in downtown Lima. A further boost occurred when Enrique Solari Swayne received international recognition for his play *Collacocha* (1955), a popular work that brought to the stage the struggle between humans and the hostile forces of nature in the Peruvian Andes. *Collacocha* toured Latin America and Spain and made Solari Swayne a canonical name in Peruvian theater; it also made Luis Alvarez, the actor who played the protagonist, Echecopar, one of Peru's most popular names on the stage.

Sebastián Salazar Bondy continued to be a major figure in Peruvian theater in the 1950s as playwright, director, critic, and artistic adviser. With the help of the Ministry of Education, he reorganized its theatrical division and was instrumental in the founding of the Club de Teatro de Lima group, directed by Reynaldo D'Amore. After receiving the National Theater Award in 1947, he went on to write nine more plays and a number of brief one-act plays. Salazar Bondy wrote two historical pieces, *Rodil* (1954), based on the life of General Rodil, the protagonist of Spain's last stand against independence, and *Flora Tristán* (1959), which evoked the life of a French-Peruvian woman who was a feminist and defender of worker's rights in the nineteenth century. He also authored two social dramas, *No hay isla feliz* (There Is No Island of Happiness; 1954) and *Algo que quiere morir* (Something Wishes to Die; 1956). In addition, he wrote satirical comedies such as *El fabricante de deudas* (The Debt-Maker; 1963) and *La escuela de los chismes* (School for Gossip; 1965). Shortly before his premature death in 1965, Salazar Bondy published *El rabdomante* (The Sorcerer), considered by many his best piece. A one-act play, the work takes issue with the artist's position in society. In the play, the inhabitants of a remote community suffer from a long drought, the symbol of social injustice, until a water diviner, representing the figure of the artist, shows them how to find water for themselves. Shortly after, they rise up and kill their rulers, including their benefactor. Perhaps inspired by the then-young Cuban Revolution, *El rabdomante* sees the artist as a promoter of revolutionary values, but is realistic enough to realize that, as a product of the middle classes, the artist is also condemned to become a victim of the same revolution he or she has helped promote. For *El rabdomante* Salazar Bondy was posthumously awarded the National Theater Award in 1965.

The theatrical wealth of the 1950s was further nurtured by outstanding visitors such as the Teatro de la Universidad Católica de Chile Company (1951) and the Jean Louis Barrault Company (1955). Other visitors included the British playwright J. B. Priestley, Thornton Wilder, who became a member of AAA, Marcel Marceau, and Jean Darcante. Binational groups also joined in this theatrical fever: the Good Companions sponsored by the British Council, the Theater Workshop sponsored by the Instituto Cultural Peruano-Norteamericano, and continuous openings at the Alliance Française, all performing in their respective languages.

## The 1960s

The momentum gained by Peruvian theater during the 1950s continued in the 1960s as new theater groups were formed and as playwrights started to receive important international recognition. In 1960, the Teatro de la Universidad Católica (Theater of the Catholic University), known as TUC, was created, headed by Ricardo Blume, one of Peru's most distinguished directors and actors. Blume's role in the development of the contemporary Peruvian theater would prove to be very influential, giving birth to a more professional and international theater. While directing many classic pieces by Pirandello, Cervantes, and Goldoni and Oswaldo Dragún, as well as the works of contemporary Peruvian playwrights such as Juan Larco, Julio Ortega, and Sarina Helfgott, Blume also worked with a number of young actors who would later become important names in Peruvian theater, including Saby Kamalich, Alberto Isola, Hernán Romero, and Elva Alcandré, among others.

Also important during this time are playwright Sara Joffré and actor Aurora Colina, who formed the Homero Teatro de Grillos (Homer Cricket Theater) group, staging a number of foreign plays, including many works from Ionesco's Theater of the Absurd. Joffré and Colina can also be credited for their important contributions to children's theater during this time. The mime Jorge Acuña was also responsible for the creation of the Teatro de la Calle (Street Theater), bringing popular theater to the streets for the first time.

As Peruvian theater grew reaching new and more sophisticated audiences, a number of theater companies visited Lima in the 1960s. Such is the case of the Old Vic Theater from London, with Vivien Leigh playing the lead in *Camille*, and Jean Vilar with his legendary Popular Theater of France, which staged Molière's *Don Juan*. Also, Vittorio Gassman, who performed *Orestes*, by Alfieri, and *The Game of Heroes*, an amazing solo performance with Gassman interpreting a parade of heroes. The famed Uruguayan director of the El Galpón Theater (Hut Theater), Atahuallpa del Cioppo, worked with Peruvian artists staging a production of *The Threepenny Opera*, underscoring the importance of Bertolt Brecht in contemporary theater. The Spaniard Juan Osuna directed Elvira Travesí and Alfredo Bouroncle in *La Celestina* by Fernando de Rojas.

A number of playwrights helped energize Peruvian theater as well. An important play of this period was Julio Ramón Ribeyro's *Vida y pasión de Santiago el pajarero* (Life and Passion of Santiago, the Birdman), written in 1958 and premiered in 1960. Hugely popular with audiences, the play is based on a story by Ricardo Palma in which an eighteenth-century visionary believes he has discovered the secret of flight. Ribeyro adapts Palma's original version in order to portray the protagonist, Santiago, as an individual of artistic creativity and quixotic idealism for, ultimately, the play is a poignant commentary on the marginal situation of the artist in contemporary society. In 1969, Alonso Alegría's *El cruce sobre el Niagara* (Crossing over the Niagara) won the prestigious Casa de las Américas drama award in Cuba. Alegría's play is based on the exploits of Blondin, a nineteenth-century French tightrope walker known for having crossed the Niagara Falls on a wire on several occasions. In the play, Blondin, a 45-year-old man of the circus, has as his counterpart the character of Carlo, an adolescent member of the circus who sees Blondin as his hero. Carlo soon accuses Blondin of having become a commercial showman and urges him to attempt more challenging endeavors using his physical talents. In this context, the Niagara Falls are a symbol of the abyss of existential emptiness, as well as a test of human courage. While Blondin and Carlo function at first as opposites, the test of crossing the Falls as a single being, re-creating the figure of Icarus, is a triumphant allegory of human mental and physical powers to endure.

Other important works by Peruvian playwrights during this period include Gregor Díaz's *Los del 4* (The Clan in Apartment 4; 1967); Sara Joffré's *Cuento alrededor de un círuclo de espuma* (Story Around a Circle of Foam; 1962); César Vega Herrera's *Ipacankure* (Ipacankure, 1968), which received the Casa de las Américas award; and actor and director Hernando Cortés's *La Ciudad de los Reyes* (City of Kings; 1967).

**The 1970s**

While many of the established theater groups such as AAA continued to stage high-quality plays, and new groups, such as Telba, directed by Jorge Guerra, were created, the most important developments in Peruvian theater in the 1970s were influenced by the new political spirit of the decade. Inspired by Grotowski's Poor Theater, a socially committed school of theater that flourished in Communist Poland, and resorting primarily to the body instead of text in their productions, Yuyachkani and Cuatrotablas (Four Stages) rose as dominant popular theater groups. Theirs was a full-time theater, and members adopted an almost monastic lifestyle, where theatrical creation was a way of life. During this period, the influence of the Cuban Revolution and a left-wing military regime in Peru, led by General Juan Velasco Alvarado, brought political awareness to a certain type of theater that began using the stage to reflect on social conditions. The notion of *creación colectiva*, or collective creation, as an expression of collective conscience, set aside the selfish and theocratic space of the author. Such socially committed theater eventually led to the organization of the National Theater Encounters (Encuentros Nacionales de Teatro), coordinated by Sara Joffré, Jorge Guerra, and Ernesto Ráez, among others, a project that would continue through the 1990s. Influenced by the teachings of Brecht, this was not only an analytical theater that chose its means of expression and adapted it to a new philosophy of representation, it also defined art by its effectiveness in portraying a political vision of society. Popular theater also focused on financially and administratively stewarding the mobilization and staging in various provincial capitals of Peru hundreds of theater groups, both from the capital and the provinces. For the first time, theater reached all kinds of audiences in Peru, serving as a tool to reflect on the many problems of Peruvian social reality.

However, all the creative energy that prompted collective theater began to slowly decline by the late 1970s as a result of political changes in the country, namely the demise of the military regime. In terms of artistic sensitivity, it would seem that actors who engaged in collective projects had drained all the imagination their bodies had to offer or had discovered that the written word is less perishable than pure gesture. Nevertheless, Yuyachkani and Cuatrotablas continue to be important participants in Peru's contemporary theater.

**The 1980s**

By the 1980s, Peruvian theater returned to the protagonism of the author and the director, while a new generation of actors, directors, and playwrights also emerged. The many political events of the 1980s—the return to democracy under President Belaúnde, hyperinflation, and the rise of left-wing guerrilla groups such as Shining Path and the Movimiento Revolucionario Túpac Amaru—also redefined many popular theater groups' political commitment. A new group, Quinta Rueda (Fifth Wheel), led by Ruth Escudero, Violeta Cáceres, and Cecilia Natteri, concerned itself with women's issues. The group Alondra (Lark) was founded by Celeste Viale and Jorge Chiarella, and Ensayo (Rehearsal) was founded by Luis Peirano, Alberto Isola, and Jorge Chiarella. In addition to Yuyachkani and Cuatrotablas, which opened important schools to train new actors and directors, a new popular theater group, La Tarumba (Bewilderment), was formed by Fernando Zevallos and Estela Paredes. Also important was the work of the actor Edgar Guillén, who staged a number of plays based on the concept of the monologue, producing interesting artistic results.

The return of the author and the director also led to the creation of the *Movimiento Independiente de Teatro (MOTIN)*, or Independent Theater Movement, in 1985, which during the course of the last 17 years years attained amazing achievements both on and off stage. While keeping alive its intention to make theater available to all throughout Peru, MOTIN also attempted to organize all existing theater groups in the hopes of improving their artistic and professional development. For a while, MOTIN proved to be a useful project, managing to attract as many as 165 theater groups throughout Peru, and became a window for better international exposure of Peruvian theater.

Several new trends characterized theater productions in the 1980s, particularly the free adaptations of literary works. Such is the case of Juan Larcos's *Ubú Presidente* (Ubú President), based on Alfred Jarry's *Ubú Rey*, performed by the Teatro de la Universidad Católica. Young directors and playwrights like José Enrique Mavila also adapted Shakespeare's *The Tempest*, and Luis Felipe Ormeño brought to the stage Manuel Puig's *The Kiss of the Spider Woman* and Mario Vargas Llosa's novel *Los cachorros* (The Cubs).

A number of playwrights also decided to direct their own plays such as Juan Rivera Saavedra, whose piece *Ahí viene Pancho Villa* (Pancho Villa Is Coming), staged by the group Alondra, enjoyed much success in the mid-1980s. Also important were the many plays staged by the group Ensayo under the direction of Alberto Isola, Luis Peirano, and Jorge Guerra. Managing to stage an average of three plays a year, Ensayo maintained a high level of quality in its productions as a result of good academic and practical knowledge of theater. Some of its most memorable performances include Brecht's *The Good Woman of Setzuan*, José María Rodríguez Méndez's *Bodas que fueron famosas del Pingajo y la Fandanga* (Famous Marriages of Pingajo and Fandanga), and the adaptation of Euripides's *The Bacchantes.*

Another important adaptation was Peter Elmore's *Encuentro de Zorros* (Encounter of Foxes) in 1985, based on José María Arguedas's work *El zorro de arriba y el zorro de abajo* and performed by Yuyachkani. Yuyachkani also enjoyed remarkable success with *Los músicos ambulantes* (Travelling Musicians), a play widely performed on streets, plazas, and theaters in Peru and abroad in 1983.

A major event in Peruvian theater was the publication of three plays by the country's most important novelist, Mario Vargas Llosa. He published *La señorita de Tacna* (The Young Lady from Tacna; 1981) and *Kathie y el hipopótamo* (Kathie and the Hippopotamus; 1983), two pieces that dwell on art and the power of creativity. They were both performed by Argentine companies in Lima and other cities in Latin America, enjoying good commercial success. In 1986, Vargas Llosa's third play, *La Chunga,* premiered in Lima. Directed by Luis Peirano of the group Ensayo, it starred one of Peru's most talented actresses, Delfina Paredes, in the role of La Chunga. Julio Ramón Ribeyro also returned to the stage with a historical play set in the central Andes, *Atusparia* (1981).

New works by young playwrights in the theater of this period include José Enrique Mavila's *Camino de rosas* (A Road of Roses; 1985) and Alfonso Santisteban's historical play *El caballo del Libertador* (The Horse of the Libertador; 1986). Santisteban would continue his active role in Peruvian theater in the 1990s as director of the group Teatrotrés (Three Theater). Among other works, he would publish the important play *Vladimir* in 1994.

### The 1990s

As Peru slowly overcame the scars of the long period of violence begun in 1980 by Shining Path, whose leader Abimael Guzmán was captured in 1992 under the new government of President Fujimori, theater continued to grow in many directions during the 1990s. Despite strong competition from other forms of entertainment such as cable television and movie videos, and the country's financial hardships, which made promotion of the genre difficult, many groups showed a return to the production of classical plays, while younger artists explored new artistic possibilities.

The Escuela Nacional de Arte Escénico, under the direction of Ruth Escudero, continued to promote theater both in Lima and other cities in Peru. It once again staged a number of Peruvian classics, including Enrique Solari Swayne's *Collacocha,* César Vega Herrera's *Ipacankure,* and Julio Ramón Ribeyro's *Santiago, el pajarero,* while also producing new plays such as *Qoillur*

*Ritti* (Lord of the Snow) by Delfina Paredes. More important, the ENAE sponsored a number of contests in search of new talent, giving notoriety to new playwrights such as Eduardo Adrianzén, author of *El día de la luna* (Moon Day; 1996), Juan Manuel Sánchez, author of *Paralelos secantes* (Closing Parallels; 1993), and César de María, author of *El poeta, la mujer y la maleta* (The Poet, the Woman and the Suitcase; 1997).

In 1991, the Teatro de la Universidad Católica celebrated thirty years of existence by staging Strindberg's *The Ghost Sonata*. Other productions included Shakespeare's *Julius Caesar* and Aristophanes's *Lysistrata*. Especially noteworthy were the production of plays by Calderón de la Barca: *La vida es sueño* (Life Is a Dream; 1635), directed by Edgar Saba, and *El gran teatro del mundo* (The Great Theater of the World; 1633), directed by Luis Peirano. The staging of these seventeenth-century classics by Calderón de la Barca in the late 1990s on the porticos of Lima's Cathedral with a huge cast of actors rekindled an old Lima tradition dating back to the colonial period and continued by director Ricardo Roca Rey in the 1950s.

In 1998, Lima's old Teatro Municipal was destroyed by a fire. Soon thereafter a campaign was started to rebuild this landmark of Peruvian culture. The effort included a production of Shakespeare's *King Lear* by the Teatro de la Universidad Católica, which was performed among the ruins of the Teatro Municipal and was directed by Edgar Saba. The cast included a number of old and new talented actors, such as Alberto Isola, Mónica Sánchez, Salvador del Solar, Cecica Bernasconi, Roberto Moll, Carlos Victoria, and Diego Bertie. Most recently, the Universidad Católica's curriculum has been restructured in an attempt to provide better professional training to newer generations of actors and playwrights. The experience and talent of actors and directors such as Alberto Isola, Luis Peirano, and Ricardo Blume will surely produce great results.

Popular theater groups continued producing a large number of plays always exploring new artistic options. Such was the case of Yuyachkani, who organized a theater festival in the poor district of Comas in Lima, bringing new life to popular theater. Yuyachkani also staged a number of plays that addressed the issue of violence in Peruvian society such as *No me toquen ese vals* (Don't Play that Waltz to Me; 1990) and *Retorno* (The Return; 1996). In 1999, Cuatrotablas looked back at its many productions throughout the years in a show called "El Teatro Total" (Total Theater). It featured many old adaptations, including Brecht's *The Bloody Return of Arturo Ui*, and a number of individual performances such as *Niña de cera* (Wax Girl), *Canto a los Santos* (Singing to the Saints), and *Flor de primavera* (Spring Flower). Cuatrotablas recently celebrated thirty years as a theater group.

A new group called Umbral, was formed by some old members of Ensayo in 1991 with Alberto Isola as its director. Umbral continued staging a number of important productions in the 1990s. Some of these included *La gran magia* (Grand Magic) by Eduardo Defilipo; *Llega Godot* (Godot Arrives), based on Beckett's *Waiting for Godot*, *Mary Queen of Scots* by Friedrich von Schiller; and *Quintuples* (Quintuplets) by Luis Rafael Sánchez.

A number of young playwrights continue to nurture the future of Peruvian theater with many important works. Some of these talents include César de María, *Kamikaze o la historia del cobarde japonés* (Kamikaze or the Story of the Cowardly Japanese; 1990); Rafael Dumett, *Números reales* (Real Numbers; 1994); Eduardo Andrianzén, *De repente un beso* (A Sudden Kiss; 1995), *Tres amores postmodernos* (Three Post-Modern Loves; 1998) and *La tercera edad de la juventud* (Youth's Third Age; 1999); and José Castro Urioste, *Cebiche en Pittsburgh* (Cebiche in Pittsburgh; 1999), to mention a few. Also, significant are a number of plays written by women playwrights in the 1990s, including Alicia Saco, *Transitando* (In Transit; 1993) and *Sombras* (Shadows; 1998); Celeste Viale, *En un árbol sin hojas* (A Tree Without Leaves; 1991), *Zapatos de calle* (Street Shoes; 1991); and Marcela Robles, *Género Desconocido* (Unknown Gender; 1990) and *Contragolpe* (Counterpunch; 1992).

Despite its many limitations in infrastructure, theater remains an active genre in Peru's cultural scene and an important medium through which to explore Peruvian reality.

## MUSIC AND DANCE

Music in Peru comes in genres and styles as varied and unique as are the cultures that exist in its different geographical regions—the coast, the Andes, and the Amazon basin. Dating back to pre-Hispanic times, such musical diversity reflects the different communication practices and artistic sensibilities unique to each social group throughout the country.

Anthropologists estimate that music has been played and listened to in Peru for over 10,000 years. It is assumed that with the appearance of the Inca empire's more complex forms of political organization, musical activity also became more sophisticated as the ruling class incorporated it into its ceremonies and celebrations. In modern-day Peru, some pre-Hispanic instruments are still used in Andean music. The most well-known are an Indian flute, the *quena*, and a pan-pipe instrument, the *zampoña*, which is a bound cluster of sealed tubes with varying lengths to set the pitch of each note. Other foreign instruments were adapted after the arrival of the Spaniards in the sixteenth century. Such is the case of many string instruments, such as the *charango*, a type of small guitar, and the mandolin and the lute, also brought from Europe, and the harp, *arpa*, and violin, whose physical shape

Andean musician, Huánuco. Photo by Gloria Satizabal de Araneta.

and sound varies from the central Andes in Huancayo to the way it is played in the southern highlands of Ayacucho or Cuzco.

The oldest musical genre still existing in Peru is the *yaraví*. It originated from a form of Inca poetry. The lyrics of the *yaraví* are often a lament or complaint, generally regarding love, the death of a loved one, or social marginalization. The *yaraví* is not danced, only sung; it is a slow rhythm full of drama and melancholy. Women tend to sing it in the highest possible pitch, a characteristic of Andean music.

Many Andean dances are associated with ceremonies and rituals of popular origin and diverse social events of festive character. For example, the people of the highlands have a unique way of celebrating ceremonies and rituals associated with traditional rural activities (such as the harvest), as well as Catholic holidays. Consequently, each region has its own typical costumes, choreography, musical instruments, and genres. For celebrations that are not religious in nature, the most popular dance is the *huayno*, a dance of pre-Hispanic origin, but which has absorbed foreign influences in modern times. Although the basic rhythm is the same throughout the Andes, cadences and styles vary according to the area. It is danced by couples, but with no physical contact. A song that originated from Andean music is "El cóndor pasa." Better known in English as "If I Could," it was composed by Daniel Alomía Robles (1871–1942) and made popular in the 1960s by Simon and Garfunkel. Andean music has also influenced contemporary classical music. Such is the case of Celso Garrido Lecca (1926), one of Peru's most renowned composers and author of *Elegía a Machu Picchu* (Eulogy to Machu Picchu, 1965).

On the coast, where the influence of European music was more influential and where a creole culture developed with the mixture of Spanish and native blood, the Peruvian waltz, or *vals criollo*, is widely practiced. Reminiscent of the Viennese waltz of the late-nineteenth century, the *vals criollo* is danced by couples holding one hand and half-embracing the waist. Peru's coastal music is dominated by the guitar and a wooden box with a sound hole called a *cajón*, which is played with the hands and with the musician sitting on top of the instrument. The guitar is played with a special technique and is used to accompany a wide range of other rhythms. Two of Peru's most popular waltz composers were Felipe Pinglo Alva (1899–1936), author of "El plebeyo" (The Plebeian), and Chabuca Granda (1920–1983), who wrote one of the most internationally-known pieces of music, the waltz "La flor de la canela" (Cinnamon Flower).

The Peruvian coast was also the site for the development of popular black music. Afro-Peruvians are the descendents of slaves brought from Africa during the colonial period to work on sugar and coastal plantations. Because of their history, many modern Afro-Peruvian songs and dances tell of the people's working conditions, of their servitude, and of the freedom they obtained in the nineteenth century. In terms of dance, the most prominent aesthetics are the emphasis on rhythm and percussion, the counterpoint between soloists and the chorus, improvisation and melodic variation, and a great display of agility and dynamics. The most popular Afro-Peruvian genre is *festejo*. As its name indicates, the *festejo* is a festive and suggestive dance, which includes movements that allude to romantic and even sexual encounters.

With time, the influence of black music was felt on the *vals criollo* and another dance, the *marinera*, that developed on the coast during the nineteenth century. In the *vals criollo*, the black influence is evident through the incorporation of percussion instruments such as the *cajón* and an instrument made of the jawbone of a donkey or horse called the *quijada*, known for its syncopated rhythm, agile choreography, and a certain emphasis on shoulder and hip movements. A similar influence of Afro-Peruvian origin can be found in the *marinera*, a dance performed by couples that features the use of a handkerchief twirled in the hand of each dancer and a complex choreography that plays out across an orderly sequence of step movements in a synchronized fashion. In northern Peru, the *marinera* extends into other dances of greater movement, such as the festive *tondero*, also of black origin.

Afro-Peruvian music's popularity continues to grow both inside and outside Peru. In 1995, Susana Baca, an interpreter of old Afro-Peruvian music, came to world attention when producer and singer David Byrne discovered her rendition of the song "María Landó" and released it as part of a recording called *The Soul of Black Peru*. A singer for some twenty years, gifted with a splendid voice, Baca founded the Black Continuum (Instituto Negrocontinuo) in Lima, a research institute dedicated to preserving Afro-Peruvian culture. Her association with Byrne helped launch her singing career internationally, and currently she is one of Peru's most internationally known singers. Some of Baca's most recent releases include *Eco de sombras* (Shadow Echoes; 2000), *Vestida de vida* (Dressed with Life; 2000), and *Espíritu vivo* (Live Spirit; 2002).

The Amazon is the birthplace of a number of wind and percussion instruments, many of which are linked to the jungle tribes' vision of the world, their work, and their ritual ceremonies. Amazon instruments include the semiotic drums, used by Bora natives. The drum name stems from the fact that the Bora have developed a musical language capable of transmitting messages. Made from large tree trunks, these drums make communication possible over surprising distances.

The youngest of musical genres in Peru is *chicha* music, also known as Peruvian *cumbia*. *Chicha* music is hugely popular among Andean migrants all across Peru. It originated in the cities of the Amazon in the 1960s and later moved into impoverished city areas at the same time the Colombian *cumbia* became very popular in Peru. An extremely joyful dance, it is a combination of tropical rhythms blended with traditional Andean melodies.

It is played with electric guitars, percussion instruments, and drums at huge public dance halls in populous urban districts. It is danced by couples who alternately hold hands and then part.

## ROCK AND POP MUSIC IN PERU

As opposed to salsa and chicha music, rock and roll and pop music in Peru have not reached wide audiences. The beginnings of rock date back to 1955, when many local groups were influenced by the music of Elvis Presley, Bill Haley, Buddy Holly, and the Beatles. Some of the most popular rock bands of that period were Los Alfiles (The Bishops), Los Stars (The Stars), Los Atomos (The Atoms), Los Incas Modernos (The Modern Incas), and Los Zodiac's (The Zodiacs). In the mid 1960s, surf music, the go-go, and psychedelia brought about a new generation of musicians such as Los Saicos and Los Doltons.

The period between 1967 and 1974 was largely influenced by groups such as Los Shain's, Traffic Sound, and We All Together. Los Shain's featured popular musicians such as Juan Luis Pereira and Enrique Ego Aguirre—two of the best guitarists of their time—who launched popular hits such as "Tomahawk." Combining rock, psychedelia, and Latin rhythms, as in one of their best-known hits "Mescalina" (Mescalina), Traffic Sound became one of the most representative groups of Peruvian rock of the period. Another group, We All Together, emulating the style of John Lennon and Paul McCartney, became one of the best performers of soft rock with such hits as "Hey Revolution."

In 1972, a group called El Polen (Polen) created a genre that was the result of a blending between psychodelic rock and Andean music. One of its most innovative features was the use of pre-Columbian instruments, such as quenas, violins, and antaras, combined with instruments used in classic rock like the electric guitar. Another group of the same period was Pax. Pax included Spanish versions of such hits as "Radar Love," originally performed by a band well-known in the United States, Golden Earring, as well as a number of pieces belonging to British and American bands of the time.

The 1980s brought about artistic independence from foreign influences. One such case was Frágil (Fragile), who authored popular hits such as "Avenida Larco" (Larco Avenue), which described the night scene in one of Lima's most modern districts. At the same time, Lima began producing new underground and punk movements. Bands such as Narcosis (Narcosis), Zcuela Cerrada (Closed School), and Leuzemia (Leukemia) were highly critical of the establishment in their lyrics, voicing a widespread discontent during one of Peru's worst periods of economic and political unrest.

In the 1990s, a wide variety of musical styles shared the Peruvian music scene along with other Latin American and Spanish rock bands. One of the most popular names of this period was Miki Gonzales. While Gonzales's early pieces of the 1980s were mostly in line with conventional rock tastes of that period, during the 1990s he performed a new type of music known as ethno-pop. Songs such as "Liberaron a Mandela" (Mandela Was Set Free), "Lamento negro" (Black Lament), and "Chicle, cigarrillos, caramelos" (Gum, Cigarettes and Candy) became popular among rock lovers. However, it was the blending of black Peruvian rhythms (such as *festejo* and *landó*) with rock, blues, calypso, and reggae music that placed Gonzales at the forefront of the local rock scene with hits such as "A gozar sabroso" (Let's Have Fun).

Other popular groups of this period are bands such as Los Nosequién Los Nosecuánto (The Idontknowwho and Howmany). Much of the popularity of this group is based on the witty blending of humor and political satire in their lyrics, as well as the fusion of light rock with salsa, rap, and ballads. One of its most popular hits was "Las Torres" (The Towers).

An important musician at the present time is Pedro Suárez-Vértiz, who became noticed as a member of the band Arena Hash in the late 1980s. In the 1990s, he launched a career as a soloist with hits such as "No existen técnicas para olvidar" (There Are No Techniques to Forget), and "Degeneración actual" (Present Degeneration). Suárez-Vértiz is considered one of the most popular and versatile Peruvian musicians, thanks to a fresh funk style with rock guitar.

With rare exceptions, rock bands have limited access to commercial radio in Peru. Their work, mostly known by performing at concerts, is largely ignored by the local recording industry. Nevertheless, new groups such as Los Mojarras, from the popular district of El Agustino in Lima, continue to appear. Los Mojarras's music blends rock and chicha rhythms, reaching wide audiences thanks to songs such as "Cachuca" and "Sarita Colonia." Another talented musician is Rafo Ráez, known for "Educación para el desempleo" (Education for Unemployment) and "El loco y la sucia" (The Crazy and the Dirty Woman). Ráez has blended punk rebelliousness with lyrics, which often portray the existential concerns of discontent urban youths. Such is also the case of Mar de Copas (Sea of Cups), heavily influenced by Spanish pop music of the 1990s. Also noteworthy is the musician Jorge "Pelo" Madueño and his band, La Liga del Sueño (League of Dreams). Although Madueño has only recorded one album, *Al derecho y al revés* (Backwards and Forward; 1994), his lyrics are considered among the best in the current rock scene.

As a whole, Peru's immense wealth of music and dance reflect its thousand-year-old culture. Moreover, its many artistic expressions are the product of an ethnically diverse and rich society.

## References

Angeles, Roberto, and José Castro-Urioste, eds. *Dramaturgia peruana.* Lima-Berkeley: Latinoamericana Editores, 1999.

Baca, Susana, Francisco Basili, and Ricardo Pereira. *Del fuego y del agua.* Lima: Pregón Editora, 1992.

Balta Campbell, Aída. *Historia general del teatro en el Perú.* Lima: Universidad de San Martín de Porres, 2001.

Bedoya, Ricardo. *100 años de cine en el Perú.* Lima: Universidad de Lima/Instituto de Cooperación Iberoamericana, 1992.

———. *Un cine reencontrado: Diccionario ilustrado de las películas peruanas.* Lima: Universidad de Lima, 1997.

———. *Entre fauces y colmillos: Las películas de Francisco Lombardi.* Huesca, Spain: Festival de Cine de Huesca, 1997.

———. *Imágenes del cine en el Perú.* Lima: Banco Central de Reserva del Perú/CONACINE, 1999.

Bonilla, George. History of Peruvian rock (1955 to 1980). Lazarus Audio Products. http://www.incarock.com/inca rock/iranth/anth2.htm. 1995. February 09, 2002.

Collazos, Yadi, Sara Joffré, Ricardo Morante, and María Reina, eds. *El libro de la muestra de teatro peruano.* Lima: Lluvia Editores, 1997.

Cornejo Guinassi, Pedro. *Juegos sin fronteras: Aproximaciones al rock contemporáneo.* Lima: El Santo Oficio, 1994.

Estenssoro, Juan Carlos. *Música y sociedad coloniales: Lima, 1680–1830.* Lima: Editorial Colmillo Blanco, 1989.

Huayhuaca, Jose Carlos. *El enigma de la pantalla.* Lima: Universidad de Lima, 1989.

———. *Hombres de la frontera: ensayos sobre cine, literatura y fotografía.* Lima: Pontificia Universidad Católica del Perú, 2001.

Hurtado, Wilfredo. *Chicha peruana: Música de los nuevos migrantes.* Lima: ECO, 1995.

King, John. *Magical Reels: A History of Cinema in Latin America.* New York: Verso, 1990.

Lloréns, José Antonio. *Música popular en Lima: Criollos y andinos.* Lima: Instituto de Estudios Peruanos/Instituto Indigenista Interamericano, 1983.

Millones, Luis. *Actores de altura: Ensayos sobre el teatro popular andino.* Lima: Editorial Horizonte, 1992.

Morris, Robert J. *The Contemporary Peruvian Theatre.* Lubbock: Texas Tech University Press, 1977.

Natella, Arthur. *The New Theatre of Peru.* New York: Senda Nueva, 1982.

Pick, Zuzana M. *The New Latin American Cinema.* Austin: University of Texas Press, 1993.

Ramos-García, Luis. "El discurso de la memoria teatral peruana en los noventa." *Latin American Theatre Review* 34, no. 1 (Fall 2000): 173–192.

Romero, Raúl. "Peru." *The Garland Handbook of Latin American Music*, ed. Dale A. Olsen and Daniel E. Sheehy. New York: Garland, 2000: 352–375.

Romero, Raúl, ed. *Música, danza y máscaras en los Andes*. Lima: Pontificia Universidad Católica del Perú/Instituto Riva Aguero, Proyecto de Preservación de la Música Tradicional Andina, 1993.

Salazar del Alcázar, Hugo. *Teatro y violencia: Una aproximación al teatro peruano de los 80*. Lima: Centro de Documentación y Video Teatral/Jaime Campodónico Editor, 1990.

Santa Cruz Gamarra, César. *El waltz y el valse criollo*. Lima: Instituto Nacional de Cultura, 1977.

Schwartz, Ronald. *Latin American Films, 1932–1994*. Jefferson, NC, and London: McFarland & Company Inc. Publishers, 1997.

Silva-Santisteban, Ricardo, ed. *Antología del teatro peruano I: Teatro Quechua*. Lima: Pontificia Universidad Católica del Perú, 2000.

———. *Antología del teatro peruano II: Teatro Colonial Siglos XVI–XVII*. Lima: Pontificia Universidad Católica del Perú, 2001.

———. *Antología del teatro peruano III: Teatro Colonial Siglo XVIII*. Lima: Pontificia Universidad Católica del Perú, 2001.

———. *Antología del teatro peruano IV: Teatro Republicano Siglo XIX*. Lima: Pontificia Universidad Católica del Perú, 2001.

———. *Antología del teatro peruano V: Teatro Republicano Siglo XX–1*. Lima: Pontificia Universidad Católica del Perú, 2002.

Sotomayor Roggero, Carmela. *Panorama y tendencias del teatro peruano*. Lima: CONCYTEC, 1990.

Tamayo Vargas, August. *Literatura peruana I, II, III*. Lima: PEISA, 1992.

Trelles, Plazaola Luis. *South American Cinema: Dictionary of Filmmakers*. Río Piedras: University of Puerto Rico, 1989.

Turino, Thomas. *Moving Away from Silence: Music of the Peruvian Altiplano and the Experience of Urban Migration*. Chicago: University of Chicago Press, 1993.

Vargas Llosa, Mario. *Mario Vargas Llosa: Three Plays*. New York: Hill & Wang, 1990.

Villagómez, Alberto. "Tendencias en el teatro peruano actual." *Conjunto* 70 (1986): 33–41.

# 7

# Art, Architecture, and Photography

## PAINTING

### Colonial Art

DURING PRE-HISPANIC TIMES, art was a major endeavor of the pre-Columbian people. Their painted pottery and textiles are admired in museums in Peru and abroad. However, the arrival of the Spanish conquistadors in the sixteenth century imposed a new set of artistic values, as well as new styles and approaches to art.

Colonial painting was mainly a religious affair, and artists usually used educational rather than aesthetic themes in their works. The purpose was to introduce the newly integrated population to Christian traditions and beliefs. Painting had to express in the clearest way possible the new Hispanic perspective. Such an intention was even more important in a society in which both conquerors and conquered were largely illiterate.

The two main branches of Peruvian colonial painting began at the same time in Lima and Cuzco. Initially, Italian masters such as the Jesuit Bernardo Bitti, and later Angelino Medoro and Mateo Pérez de Alesio, introduced the European Manneristic School, followed in the seventeenth century by the Flemish Jesuit Van den Brugen, who in Peru changed his name to Diego de la Puente.

Soon after the European masters established the basis for Christian Peruvian art, local Indian and mestizo masters began to produce paintings of great quality, especially in the Cuzco School of Art, or Escuela Cuzqueña, whose development and history reflects that of Cuzco itself. In the late sixteenth and early seventeenth century, artists such as Gregorio Gamarra and Lázaro Pardo de Lagos represented Spanish Mannerism with local influences. By the mid-seventeenth century, however, a few masters developed a new style, the most renowned of which was Diego Quispe Tito, who mixed the Spanish Baroque and fading Mannerism with local motifs in what was called the Cuzquenian Baroque.

During the eighteenth century, the end of colonial times expresses a change in mentality and the development of a more national approach, where the white-and-pink saints and cherubs give way to darker madonnas and angels in what was called the Popular Cuzquenian School. Some artists of this time have purely Indian names such as Marcos Zapaca or Antonio Wilca. During this later period, murals with strong Andean influences appear in convents and private homes, a branch of Peruvian arts that currently attracts great interest.

### The Early Nineteenth Century

With the advent of independence and the collapse of the colonial regime, there were new ideas in almost every aspect of life, and art was no exception. Once free from Spain, the first decades of Peruvian national life gave birth to two artistic styles. The first imitated the portraits of many momentous figures that political change had produced in the rest of the world. José Gil de Castro (1783–1841), a talented mulatto who lived in Peru and Chile, painted portraits of Peru's important political protagonists of those years. Born in Lima in 1783, Gil de Castro went to Chile in his early years and became a part of the liberation army headed by General José de San Martín, with whom he collaborated as a cosmographer and cartographer. Back in Lima after the independence of the 1820s, he continued his career with great success and had a comfortable life dedicated to his profession. Although he also painted the ladies of Limenian society of the times, he is remembered as the painter of the Libertadores, that is, the generals who accompanied Generals San Martín and Bolívar during the wars of independence. Francisco Fierro, best known as Pancho Fierro (1807–1879), represents a second style that the experts call *Costumbrismo*, which tries to preserve without great academic knowledge the character, dress, and costumes of the first decades of the republic. Fierro left a wide collection of small and vivid watercolors. His genius exhibits different everyday people of those early days: salesmen, priests and nuns, civil servants, market women, dancers, soldiers on a horse, bullfights, and processions. Usually flat, single-plane illustrations, without much backdrop, Fierro's paintings are nevertheless full of color and expression, representing a vivid reflection of the Peru he saw. In fact, his works are not only pieces of art but historic social documents as well.


## Academicism

After independence in the 1820s, Academicism characterized the work of most of the well-educated Peruvian artists, who received their formal training according to academic styles of the times in Europe. In fact, they spent most of their lives in Europe and, if they ever returned to Peru, they stayed for a short amount of time during which they confirmed that it would be impossible to live in their country and dedicate themselves entirely to their craft as they were doing in Europe. In any case, their clients, the Peruvian elite, preferred to purchase their paintings directly from Europe through specialized merchants, rather than spend their money on the works of unknown nationals.

The case of Ignacio Merino (1817–1876) is typical of artists of the period. Merino left Peru at a young age and studied painting in Paris. When he returned, he taught painting and drawing at an old art school created during colonial times, and became its director for a short time. However, he realized that his future, if he wanted to continue his artistic life, was in France, and soon returned to Paris. Another case is that of Francisco Laso (1823–1869), who in Paris painted Peruvian themes from the notes he had taken while he was still living in Peru. Laso is the only example of a Peruvian artist living in Europe portraying national themes.

At the end of the nineteenth century, certain European-based artists adopted some elements of the new artistic trends. Carlos Baca Flor (1867–1941), for example, though very successful with portraits in Europe, experimented with Impressionism, and though he never worked much in natural outdoor settings, his canvases made in New York's Bronx are well crafted. However, it is Daniel Hernández (1888–1957) who can be credited as a major artistic influence in the development of twentieth-century Peruvian painting. After studying in Lima at an early age, he traveled to France, Italy, and Spain, where he came in contact with the Spanish Impressionist trend. Finally, he moved to Paris where he resided for many years and, in 1900, won a gold medal at the Universal Exposition in Paris. In 1918, Hernández returned to Peru with a government contract to organize and direct the recently established National School of Fine Arts, a post he kept until the end of his life. In addition to educating a new generation of artists, Hernández dedicated his time to the painting of historical themes, as well as portraits of the Limenian ladies of his time.

### The Indigenists

The twentieth century brought a new interest in Peruvian themes. Indigenist literature portrayed national themes, folklore, and indigenous exploitation, and played a major ideological role alongside the political currents of the time. Painters did not remain uninterested, and a rich pictorial development was started by José Sabogal (1888–1957), who early on had enriched his education with the techniques and themes of the so-called Spanish Regionalists. He also brought about a new artistic perspective that developed into the creation of an authentic Peruvian style. Sabogal's Indigenism tried to blend indigenous and Spanish elements of Peruvian culture. At first, a very conservative society found it difficult to accept his art, but ultimately his artistic ideas were followed by many students who called themselves the Grupo de los Indigenistas (Indigenist Group). The group included well-known names such as Julia Codesido (1892–1979), Enrique Camino Brent (1909–1960), Camilo Blas (1903–1986), and Carlota (Cota) Carvallo (1903–1980). These painters were sometimes accused of being too rigid in their representation of Andean reality, but their ideas were adopted and developed by other younger painters, among them Jorge Vinatea Reinoso (1900–1931), whose death in 1931 at a young age frustrated what promised to be a prolific career.

The Indigenista Movement was accepted officially in 1932, and Sabogal was appointed as the second director of the National School of Fine Arts. By that time, the Indigenist Movement had been surpassed by a new and younger group of artists, more in harmony with a country that was living its industrial revolution. By the late 1930s and early 1940s, a group that called itself the *Independientes*, well in touch with international artistic currents, began to organize exhibits. The *Independientes* had neither a fixed style nor a set of artistic principles, but they pursued new artistic alternatives and languages with which to express protest and renovation. Three facts that marked a more experimental approach in Peruvian painting were the return to Peru of Ricardo Grau (1907–1970), who had lived most of his youth in Paris, the rise of the Avant-garde movement in Europe in the 1920s, and the end of Sabogal as director of the National School of Fine Arts.

Grau gave the National School a new spirit, and students looked to him for new contacts with the Avant-garde currents that were being developed in Europe. Now students could develop their artistic expression without the rigid framework of *indigenismo*.

Considered by many as the greatest painter of the century in Peru, Sérvulo Gutiérrez (1914–1961) was a multifaceted man who, while creating fine pieces of art, also imitated pre-Hispanic ceramics that fooled even the experts. As a painter, Sérvulo, as he was popularly known, spent many years in Buenos

"Paisaje Serrano," by Enrique Camino Brent. Photo by Gloria Satizabal de Araneta. Collection of Eduardo Dargent.

Aires and Paris, where he adopted a unique style with strong influences of expressionism in which color led over form.

The *Independientes* of the 1940s gave way to the Abstractionists, and not only the younger artists but some of the old painters, such as Ricardo Grau, Juan Manuel Ugarte Eléspuru (1911–1998), Sabino Springett (1913), and Alberto Dávila (1914–1988), worked hard in the Peruvianization of this international style. Their efforts finally met with great success in 1958 at a collective exhibition of abstract art in Lima. As time went by, abstract painters adopted more and more national motifs. Fernando de Szyszlo (1923–   ), one of Peru's most internationally renowned painters, was among the most important artists of this new current. De Szyszlo's artistic vision successfully combines elements of European abstractionism with colors, forms, and textures that originate in pre-Columbian art.

A number of painters who graduated from both the National School of Fine Arts and the Art School of the Pontificia Universidad Católica del Perú

from the 1950s on, produced a well-developed vanguard group that constantly sought new forms of expression, among them Tilsa Tsuchiya, David
Herskovitz, Carlos Revilla, Herman Braun Vega, Ramiro Llona, Gerardo
Chávez, Leoncio Villanueva, and José Tola. Similarly, talented painters from
younger generations constantly produce new forms of art in Lima and in
other Peruvian cities. Some of these include Eduardo Tokeshi, Luz Letts,
Moiko Yaker, Mariví Arregui, Luis Alberto León, and Javier Ruzo, to list
only a few.

## ARCHITECTURE

Pre-Columbian architecture in Peru achieved incredible heights, second
to none. Such splendor can be seen at the temple of Kotosh, or The Crossed
Hands, in Huánuco in the central Andes (c. 1800 B.C.); the temple of Sechín
in Ancash, with its small monoliths (also from the second millennium B.C.);
and the ceremonial complex of Chavín de Huantar, also found in Ancash
(begun around 1000 B.C.), with its embellished columns, its obelisks, and
anthropomorphic heads, all cast in stone, the most striking pieces being the
noted "Lanzón de Chavín," the so-called "Estela Raimondi," and the "Ob-
elisco Tello," three of the most impressive works of Peruvian art. Likewise,
the pyramids of the Sun and the Moon in La Libertad contain scintillating
reliefs and painted murals of the Mochica culture (A.D. 300 to 900); and
Chan-Chan, capital of the kingdom of Chimú in northern Peru (which flourished from the thirteenth to the fifteenth centuries B.C.), the largest city of
clay in the world, having numerous cyclopean constructs of the Inca. In
Cuzco itself, pre-Columbian architecture is best exemplified by the fortress
of Sascayhuamán, the Coricancha, or Temple of the Sun, Ollantaytambo,
and the world-famous walled city of Machu Picchu, breathtakingly merged
into the majesty of the Andean landscape.

The establishment of new cities by the Spanish, a process which began in
1532, initially followed Renaissance models, although manifesting traces of
the Gothic period, with echoes of the Middle Ages still resonating in the
peninsula. The synthesis of these art forms with elements of indigenous culture congealed in the seventeenth century in a style known as the mestizo
Baroque, which, with Arequipa as its axis, spread through the valley of Colca
and the region of Lake Titicaca, culminating with singular mastery in Cuzco.
This style endows Peruvian cities with a unique flavor and bears witness to
the aesthetic sumptuousness of the golden years of the viceroyalty and the
immeasurable wealth that this period represented. Examples include the decorative porticos and façades of churches and monasteries, the reflections in
the vestries and altarpieces, the vaults and patios of the palaces and homes,

Machu Picchu. Photo by Gloria Satizabal de Araneta.

the finely carved balconies, the meticulously cast bars of the windows, the flat surfaces of the walls flanking city streets, and the fountains and street lamps adorning the quaint plazas. Cuzco preserves the best examples of its colonial glory: the façade of the convent and the church of the Jesuits, the central nave of the city's cathedral, the first cloister of La Merced, and the

City Hall, Lima. Photo by Gloria Satizabal de Araneta.

interior of the Palacio del Almirante. But the gracefulness of the mestizo Baroque stands out everywhere: the convent and the church of the Jesuits (Arequipa), the Palace of Torre Tagle (Lima), the church of Pomata (Puno), the interior of the temple of Belén (Cajamarca), and the interior of the cathedral (Ayacucho). All of these masterpieces capture the essence of an art form in which "the sensibilities of Andalusian Baroque, and the *churrigueresco* (an ornate Spanish Baroque style) converge, in an elegant but restrained fashion, with the local flavor of the indigenous cultures and also with the esthetic qualities of the materials used in housing construction" (Velarde 1978, 246).

Independence heralded a rejection of the colonial style of architecture and the concomitant abandoning of forms that had previously held sway. On the coast, and especially in Lima, creole techniques utilizing adobe and a type of reed work called *quincha* gave life to sparkling and elegant façades. Symmetry was expressed in a reserved Classical style. The last three decades of the nineteenth century witnessed a plethora of diverse styles, with French influences predominating. A combination of academic and eclectic currents left its imprint on local architecture.

After 1920, a transition to modern forms gradually became more apparent. In the 1930s and 1940s, contemporary trends in architecture merged with the Peruvian neocolonial style, noted for its exquisite good taste and aversion to gaudiness. Today, traditional design has lost ground to North American

District of Miraflores. Photo by Gloria Satizabal de Araneta.

emphases on purely functional towering buildings, which continue to multiply across the urban landscape of Peru.

## SCULPTURE

Peruvian sculpture initially sprang from the creative sensibilities prevalent in peninsular works. For this reason, it is important to first understand the characteristics of sculpture in Spain during the sixteenth-century period of discovery and conquest of the Americas.

The motifs of Spanish sculpture during the Renaissance reflect a strong Flemish influence. In fact, much of the artistic production from that period holds a certain Gothic flavor that would never entirely disappear from artistic production in either Spain or Flanders. In the sixteenth century, Italian ideas and techniques recently introduced to Spain would be combined, under the banner of Catholic orthodoxy, with the Gothic and Mudéjar, or Arabesque, styles that had traditionally predominated. This synthesis of influences would eventually give rise to Mannerism, a style notable for its cosmopolitan style and emphasis upon creativity and free expression. Italian artists who frequently traveled to Spain played a decisive role in this development.

Spanish sculpture would reappear in Peru, but only in an ornamental fashion and mainly in the motifs of façades and other symbolic works. Mythological motifs were virtually nonexistent, and no attempts were made to integrate the new developments in painting to sculptural representation. Even works commissioned for funerals were rare. Instead, the predominant motifs were representations of Christian themes. The use of color made human figures appear more lifelike and spontaneous, an effect heightened by the graffito used in the elaboration of clothing, which reflected the use of iconographic themes and techniques. The most popular themes utilized in these religious allegories included the representation of Christlike figures, portraits of Saints, and the baby Jesus looking down benevolently on the observer.

Sculptural materials varied little from Spain to America, even though there were some differences related to the type and quality of certain items, such as marble or wood. Spanish sculptors most frequently used wood tiles, walnut, chestnut, cypress, larch, pine, and cedar, while in the Americas artisans sculpted out of pine, cedar, and mahogany. Many traditional Spanish techniques transferred to the New World, especially in regards to the use of marble, stone, wood, wood pulp, ivory, and metals. All of these supplemented the use of maguey, a material traditionally favored by the Indians that blended well with Spanish techniques in the elaboration of wood pulp. Maguey allowed artists to reduce costs, especially in outlying regions of the Andes where cedar was not abundant. It is not unusual to find images in these regions that combine a body of maguey with hands and a head made of cedar, which was considered a more pristine and edifying material in the representation of religious figures. In Lima, wood pulp was used instead of maguey.

The late sixteenth century and early seventeenth century witnessed the most intense activity regarding the production of sculpture in colonial Peru, the most impressive works included those by the Italian Jesuit Bernardo Bitti, the Spaniards Andrés Hernández and Gómez Hernández Galván, the Basque Juan Martínez de Arrona, Pedro de Vargas, a Jesuit originally from Córdoba, and many others. The work of the Sevillian School, represented by Martín de Oviedo, Pedro de Noguera, and Gaspar Ginés, also strongly influenced sculpture in the viceroyalty of Peru. The appearance of the Sevillian School's works in the middle part of the seventeenth century established norms for the school of Lima and helped it adapt to new trends in sculpture.

Among the Spanish artists who traveled to America, Gregorio Fernández, an artist from the School of Valladolid, produced exceptional pieces that include figures of San Joaquín, Santa Ana, and the Virgin as a Young Girl, all of which can be admired in the Jesuit shrine in San Pedro, one of Lima's most traditional churches. San Pedro also houses the works by the noted sculptor Pedro de Mena, originally from Granada and a disciple of Alonso Cano, a renowned Spanish painter, architect, and sculptor of the seventeenth century. *Ecce Homo* and a *Dolorosa* represent some of his pieces that appear in a façade dedicated to San Luis Gonzaga.

Notable artists who sent works to America include Melchor Caffa, although he was Maltese rather than Spanish. A disciple of the Roman School, Caffa sculpted his *Tránsito de Santa Rosa* (The Death of Santa Rosa), crafted in Carrara marble, which Pope Clement IX commissioned and was supposedly inspired by Bernini's *The Experience of Santa Teresa.*

The most notable of the numerous artists comprising the School of Lima was Pedro de Noguera. Born in Barcelona, he did his apprenticeship in Seville and in 1619 moved to Lima, where in a few years he became the supervisor of artistic endeavors at Lima's cathedral. In 1619, Noguera accepted a contract to produce a sculpture of Christ crucified for The Brotherhood of Solitude. The work evolved into a portrait of the lifeless Christ being taken down from the cross. Even today the work demonstrates the captivating realism forged by Noguera.

By the second half of the seventeenth century, workshops specializing in the making of sculpture were well established in Lima, and the city's authorities no longer needed to commission works in Spain. However, artists who worked exclusively in sculpture were rare: even Noguera showed a marked preference for architecture and construction. The influence of the Baroque would be felt more in the façades of altars and decorative pieces in gold. This would endow the architecture of Lima with a splendor that defied the numerous earthquakes afflicting the city during this period.

The superb cathedral complex of the Franciscans was inaugurated in 1674 and marked a new chapter in the evolution of the Baroque in Lima. Especially noteworthy are the stone sculptures of the main façade constructed by Manuel de Escobar, although the cathedral's most impressive works are the pews, which were designed to seat the choir and were completed in the same year that the cathedral opened to the public.

One of the most accomplished artists of the eighteenth century was the mestizo Baltazar Gavilán. Unfortunately, some of his most important pieces have been lost, including the equestrian statue of King Phillip V of Spain, which graced the threshold of the bridge erected over the Rímac River and was a casualty of the earthquake of 1746 in Lima. Among his surviving works, however, are the impressive *El arquero de la muerte* (The Archer of Death) and the *Virgen Dolorosa* (The Lamenting Virgin), whose fine outlines are accentuated by tears made of crystal.

With the advent of Peruvian independence in the early nineteenth century, many of these works were replaced by the dominating neoclassical style in the crafting of public monuments.

The equestrian statue of Simón Bolívar erected in the Plaza of the Inquisition, where it has remained from the nineteenth century until the present day, heralded a wave of sculptures commemorating the victories of Peruvian independence.

Among the various monumental works of this period, the Monument to the Dos de Mayo (Second of May) symbolizes the heroic defense of the port of Callao against the Spanish army in 1866, and has a notable urban focus. Another important work is the monument to Francisco Bolognesi, a hero of the war against Chile in the late nineteenth century, by the sculptor Artemio Ocaña.

Two important monuments were erected in Lima in the years preceding the Centennial of Peruvian Independence: the monument to President Ramón Castilla, who declared the end of slavery in Peru, by David Lozano, inaugurated in 1915; and the statue of the Italian savant Antonio Raimondi, by Ocaña, also of 1915. Unfortunately, Raimondi's statue was destroyed by a bomb. It would be rebuilt fourteen years later and inaugurated in the Paseo Colón by President Leguía during the early part of the twentieth century.

Enthusiastic celebrations greeted the Centennial of Peruvian Independence in 1921. A large wave of commemorative monuments graced parks and thoroughfares throughout Lima. Crafted by the Spanish sculptor Mariano Benlliure, a statue of General José de San Martín, one Peru's heroes in the war of independence against Spain, was inaugurated in a main plaza of downtown Lima that bears his name. Another original work was the edifice given to the city by the Italian community in Lima as a monument to 100 years of Peruvian independence. This work by the architect Gaetano Moretti is currently in the Museum of Italian Art. Belgium donated an exquisite piece by the great sculptor Constantino Meunier, *El Estibador* (The Longshoreman), which captured the harsh conditions of the working classes with moving realism. The Chinese community donated a Chinese fountain located in Exposition Park. The monument provided by the Japanese community celebrated the first Inca, Manco Cápac, as a hero of the Inca empire and stands in La Victoria, a popular district in Lima.

Gertrude Whitney sculpted the gift from the U.S. community, *La Fuente de las Tres Figuras* (The Fountain of the Three Faces). The original had previously won an honorable mention in Paris in 1913 and had gone on to take first prize the following year in a local Peruvian contest.

For its part, the Peruvian government commissioned Artemio Ocaña to erect a monument dedicated to Admiral Georges Henri du Petit Thouars, in gratitude for his intervention in the War against Chile in 1879. The government also contributed a monument to George Washington, a copy of a work by Houdon, which was erected in 1922 in the plaza that bears his name.

A disciple of the famous sculptor Auguste Rodin, the Peruvian sculptor Luis Agurto de Olaya, gained reknown for his monument to *El Soldado Desconocido* (The Unknown Soldier), located in the Solar Bluff on the coast of Lima, as well as for his embossed relief that celebrates the taking of the oath of independence, which was placed in the meeting room of the House of Deputies in the Peruvian congress in 1922.

During the last decade of the nineteenth century, Modernism arrived in Peru from various sources. Art Nouveau appeared in the first decade of the twentieth century. The works of Quispez Asín in the 1920s, and those of Joaquín Roca Rey in the 1950s would introduce more contemporary styles into Peruvian sculpture.

The Italian sculptor Eugenio Baroni's monument to Jorge Chávez, a pioneer in the history of Peruvian aviation, echoes the flight and tragic end of the Greek mythological figure of Icarus and ranks as one of the most important works of this period. The Spaniard Victorio Macho elaborates in bronze another milestone with his monument to Admiral Miguel Grau, a hero of the war against Chile.

Between 1935 and 1937, the Chinese colony commissioned two sculptures celebrating the 400th anniversary of the founding of Lima and placed them in the Paseo de la República, one of Lima's main avenues: *Las llamas* (The Llamas) by Agustín Rivera and *El Trabajo* (Hard Work), a realist piece in bronze made in homage to the Indian peasant by Ismael Pozo.

Another monumental work of the twentieth century can be found at the Campo de Marte, one of Lima's most popular parks. In reality, it reflects a melange of several pieces made in 1945 by Artemio Ocaña in memory of those who fell in the 1941 war against Ecuador. Its themes pay a moving tribute to patriotism and national pride. Other important sculptures include those done by Miguel Baca Rossi to commemorate the historical and political legacy of José Carlos Mariátegui and Víctor Raúl Haya de la Torre, two of Peru's most influential thinkers in the twentieth century, both of which can be found in downtown Lima.

Other sculptors who have made significant contributions include Cristina Gálvez, Anna Maccagno, Víctor Delfín, Alberto Guzmán, Fabián Sánchez,

Marina Núñez del Prado (who, although of Bolivian origin, lived and worked most of her life in Peru), Emilio Rodríguez Larraín, Jorge Eduardo Eielson and, most recently, Benito Rosas and Sonia Prager.

## PHOTOGRAPHY

The origin of Peruvian photography as an artistic and documentary medium dates back to the pioneering work of a number of French and American photographers who settled in Peru during the early nineteenth century. In 1842, Maximiliano Danti brought the first daguerreotype, the predecesor of the modern photograph, from France and opened the first professional studio in Lima. The new technology was received with enthusiasm, and its popularity quickly spread. Nevertheless, the use of the daguerreotype was short-lived and the photograph soon replaced it. In 1856, Emile Garreaud established an important studio specializing in portraiture. Family and celebrity portraits became increasingly popular in the 1860s when two Frenchmen, Eugene and Aquiles Courret, became reputed photographers of the Peruvian upper class. The Courret studio maintained an important influence on the local industry well into the early twentieth century as photography became a permanent feature in the newspaper and advertising industry. Along with Ricardo Villalba and the American Benjamin Franklin Pease, the Courret brothers produced a number of images of Peruvian architecture, monuments, and newly built railroads, many of which were presented during a large exhibition in Lima in 1872. Additionally, a number of American and European travelers such as George E. Squire, Thomas Hutchinson, Charles Lummis, Charles Kroehle, and Fernand Garreaud left valuable collections of images representing pre-Columbian ruins, rural and urban settings, and a variety of social characters and celebrities of the young Peruvian republic.

### Martín Chambi (1891–1973)

Peru's most famed photographer of the twentieth century is Martín Chambi. Born in a small town near Puno in the Peruvian altiplano, Chambi lived his most important years as an artist in Cuzco in the 1920s and 1930s, at a time when many intellectuals were reconsidering the role of indigenous people and culture in Peruvian society. Chambi's images are a vivid example of the spirit of the times, recording the way of life of Andean society in Cuzco and the native villages surrounding it. He gave equal attention to the colonial architecture of Cuzco and the many archaeological sites of the area. He was the first artist to photograph Machu Picchu after it was discovered by Hiram

Bingham in 1911. Popularly known as the poet of light, *el poeta de la luz,* Chambi is credited for being one of the first photographers to experiment with setting and light in the early 1920s, whether in a formal studio portrait or in a photograph of the ruins of Machu Picchu at dawn. In addition to the rich documentary content of Chambi's photographs, an extraordinary sense of composition stands out in the some 16,000 images he produced as he slowly earned an international reputation. One of his most famous photographs, "La tristeza del indio" (The Sadness of the Indian), has been republished more than 3,000 times. His work has been exhibited in most major cities in Latin America, Europe, and the United States.

### Carlos Domínguez (1933–   )

Carlos Domínguez is arguably Peru's most important living photojournalist. His work has appeared in Peru's best newspapers and weeklies, as well as in many Latin American publications. For over fifty years, Domínguez's images have captured the most crucial historical, political, social, and cultural events in Peru. He also has taken numerous classic portraits of many twentieth-century Peruvian celebrities. His images represent one of the most vivid visual samples of the complex nature of contemporary society. But whether illustrating the daily life of Peruvians in a realistic vein or the subjective nature of important social happenings, Peru's diverse society is at the core of Domínguez's images. His archive purportedly holds some 250,000 photographs, a selection of which recently appeared in a volume entitled *Los peruanos* (The Peruvians; 2000).

### Billy Hare (1946–   )

After experimenting with painting and film, Billy Hare found in photography a unique visual language influenced by the teachings of American photographers Minor White and Aaron Siskind. Thanks to the latter, he spent an extended period of time at the Rhode Island School of Design in the 1970s. The vast Peruvian landscape, from the coastal desert to the highlands, is a recurring feature in many of Hare's images. Critics have commented that the artist's need to establish a personal rapport with his homeland and its cultural traditions drives his portrayal of vast open spaces. Moreover, Hare's individual search for a personal identity through his landscapes can be read as a metaphorical search for Peru's own collective identity. His portraits often underscore the uneasy and often traumatic mix of races and pre-Columbian traditions that have survived in Peru since the Spanish conquest. Also noteworthy is Hare's interest in religious expressions. Many of his images depict crosses on roadsides, cemeteries, shrines, pre-Hispanic tombs, and the ceremonies of All Souls's Day, all of which point to the belief of something beyond immediate reality. A photographer of many talents, Hare's work has been key in the development of expressive photography in Peru.

### Javier Silva Meinel (1949– )

A professional photographer with many national and international exhibits to his credit, Javier Silva Meinel's work centers around popular celebrations and collective rituals of many sorts. A case in point is his series *Achoi Altar de Arena* (Acho: an Altar of Sand) where he elegantly portrays the ritual of bullfighting in Lima's bullring (the oldest in Latin America). However, perhaps his most well-known images deal with a number of pre-Hispanic rituals and ceremonies, as well as popular religious celebrations, both in the Peruvian highlands and the Amazon. Few photographers have so lavishly illustrated these traditional events as Silva Meinel. Many of his images stand out for their intense display of colors and for the collective emotion of the subject matter.

### Fernando La Rosa (1943– )

After earning a degree from the National School of Fine Arts in Peru, Fernando La Rosa went on to study at the Massachusetts Institute of Technology under Minor White, an influential American photographer in the 1950s. In 1976, he became president of Secuencia Cultural Association and director of Secuencia Foto Galería in Lima. He also taught photography at Armando Robles Godoy's Filmmakers School in Lima. An important feature of La Rosa's work is the juxtaposition of geometrical frame and how they alter the urban landscape. One such case can be found in the book *Photographs: Frame Series 1978–1988* (1988), in which a recurring subject matter is a window looking out to a city (New York, Atlanta, Lima). The critic Ricardo Pau-Llosa has said that in these images "La Rosa plays with multiple focuses within a single image . . . by manipulating varying degrees of transparency through which the fragments of the world are orchestrated into precision" (La Rosa 1988, 2). Many of these windows function as silent balconies or entries from which to contemplate existence. But what is striking about them is that, repeatedly, a whole range of black and white tones are included in a single image to make the world a mysterious and intriguing mirror of many realities. As Pau-Llosa comments, the photographs of La Rosa are "piercing statements about man, the small god of consciousness, and his combative, difficult glimpsing of a world finite in its translucencies, endless in its opacities" (La Rosa 1988, 2). La Rosa's work can be found in a number of museums in the United States and Europe, including the Museum of Art of the Americas in Washington, D.C., the Rhode Island Museum of Art, and the Bibliotheque National of Paris, among others. Some of his recent work centers around the images of rock in a book entitled *Neolítica* (1999). An artist of many talents, La Rosa teaches photography at Wesleyan College in Georgia.

### Roberto Huarcaya (1959–   )

After studying photography in Spain in the 1980s, Huarcaya returned to Peru where he earned a living as a professional photographer. He founded the Institute Gaudí, and later the Centro de Fotografía El Ojo Ajeno (The Other Eye Photography Center), along with Billy Hare. Some of Huarcaya's work centers around characters on the streets of Lima, such as ice-cream vendors, newspaper kiosk vendors, and shoeshiners, happily depicted in their daily routines. A more enigmatic and suggestive collection of images is entitled *La nave del olvido* (The Ship of Oblivion, 1998), where madness is the main topic. In photographing patients at a psychiatric hospital in Lima, Huarcaya explains that he worked closely with the interns, first befriending them and earning their trust, while making them familiar with what his camera did. Later, he arranged shooting sessions with a number of patients. This form of collaboration prompted a series of portraits in which patients provided a self-image, often choosing the clothing and setting in which they preferred to be photographed. Huarcaya's unique project produced a set of moving images that break away from the fear and mystery of madness, while at the same time expressing a quiet respect for the humanity of these individuals.

Other photographers that have made important contributions to the development of professional photography in Peru include Jorge Deustua, Milagros de la Torre, Luz María Bedoya, María Cecilia Piazza, Fernando Castro, Sol Toledo, Juan Enrique Bedoya, Herman Schwarz, Alejandro Balaguer, Roberto Fantozzi, Ana María McCarthy, Alicia Benavides, Mayu Mohanna, Javier Ferrand, Renzo Uccelli, Mariano Zuzunaga, Daniel Giannoni, and Flavia Gandolfo.

Pedro Campos and José Aguirre, shoe shiners in Lima. Photo by Roberto Huarcaya.

Sara Orellana Rodríguez sells religious objects in Lima. Photo by Roberto Huar-caya.

Aída Miraval Espinoza sells newspapers in Lima. Photo by Roberto Huarcaya.

## REFERENCES

Banco Central de Reserva del Perú. *Catálogo del Museo.* Introducción por Cecilia Bákula de Fosca. Lima: Banco Central de Reserva del Perú, 1984.

Camp, Roderi A. Martín Chambi Photographer of the Andes." *Latin American Research Review* 13, no. 3 (1978): 223–228.

———. "Martín Chambi Pioneer Photographer." *Américas* 3 (March 1978): 5–10.

Cossío del Pomar, Felipe. *Peruvian Colonial Art: The Cuzco School of Painting.* Trans. by Genaro Arbaiza. New York: Wittenborn, 1965.

Domínguez, Carlos. *Los peruanos.* Lima: Ed. América Leasing, 2000.

Hare, Billy. *Photographs.* Lima: Telefónica del Perú, 1997.

Heredia, Jorge. "Avatares de la obra del fotógrafo peruano Martín Chambi (1891–1973) y reseña de dos monografías recientes." *Hueso Húmero* 29 (1993): 144–176.

Huarcaya, Roberto. *The Ship of Oblivion.* Barcelona: Prismatic Arts Grafiques, 1998.

Huayhuaca, José Carlos. *Martín Chambi, fotógrafo.* Lima: Institut Français des Etudes Andines/Banco de Lima, 1991.

La Rosa, Fernando. *Photographs: Frame Series 1978–1988.* Atlanta, GA: Nexus Contemporary Art Center, 1988.

Lauer, Mirko. *Introducción a la pintura peruana del siglo XX.* Lima: Mosca Azul Editores, 1976.

———. *Szyszlo: Indagación y collage.* Lima: Mosca Azul Editores, 1975.

Lavalle, José Antonio de, ed. *Pintura contemporánea.* Lima: Banco de Crédito del Perú. Lima, 1976.

———, ed. *Pintura Virreinal.* Introducción por Juan Manuel Ugarte Eléspuru. Lima: Banco de Crédito del Peru, 1973.

López Mondéjar, Public, and Mario Vargas Llosa. *Martín Chambi 1920–1950.* Madrid: Círculo de Bellas Artes/Lunwerg Editores, 1991.

Mesa, José de Gisbert, Teresa. *Historia de la Pintura Cuzqueña I–II.* Lima: Fundación Augusto Wiese, 1982.

Ranney, Edward. "Martín Chambi Poet of Light." *Earthwatch News* 1, no. 1 (1979): 3–6.

Silva Meinel, Javier. *Acho: Altar de arena.* Lima: Unión de Cervecerías Backus y Johnston, 1992.

———. *Calendar of Peru: Fiesta Times.* Lima: Unión de Cervecarías Backus y Johnston, 1998.

———. *El libro de los encantados: Imágenes del Perú.* Lima, Unión de Cervecerías Backus y Johnston 1991.

Ugarte Eléspuru, Juan Manuel. *Pintura y escultura en el Perú contemporáneo.* Lima: Peruarte, 1970.

Velarde, Héctor. *Arquitectura peruana.* Lima: Studium, 1978.

Wild, Alfred, ed. *Fernando de Szyszlo.* Bogotá/New York: Ediciones Alfred Wild, 1991.

# Glossary

***acculturation***: A change in the cultural behavior and thinking of an individual or group through contact with another culture.

***ají***: Hot pepper.

***altiplano***: The high, flat land surrounding Lake Titicaca in Peru and Bolivia.

***anticuchos***: A dish of cubes of marinated meat similar to shish kebab.

***aprismo***: Víctor Raúl Haya de la Torre's political doctrine.

***aprista***: A member of the APRA (Alianza Popular Revolucionaria Americana) party, a center-left political organization founded by Víctor Raúl Haya de la Torre in 1924.

***apu***: A god of the mountains in Andean culture.

***arpa***: Harp.

***audiencia***: The colonial high court established in Lima during the viceroyalty of Peru.

***auqui***: The prince or heir to the Inca throne.

***auto sacramental***: A eucharistic play of Spanish origin dating back to the sixteenth century.

***ayllu***: A group of related individuals and families who exchange labor and cooperate in subsistence and ritual activities during the empire.

***Baroque***: A highly ornamental style of architecture, literature, and the arts brought from Europe by the Spaniards to the Americas in the seventeenth century.

***bijao***: Banana leaves used to wrap *juanes*.

***cajón***: A wooden box with a sound hole of Afro-Peruvian origin.

*camelid*: A member of the family that includes camels. In Peru, Andean animals such as llamas, guanacos, and alpacas belong to such a family.

*campesino*: Peasant.

*caudillo*: A politician or strongman who holds power. His authority is often based on his personal charisma rather than a democratic form of rule.

*cebiche*: A typical dish made of fish, as well as other sea products, cooked in lime juice.

*charango*: A small Andean guitar.

*chicha*: A traditional beverage made of maize. A modern form of music that blends Andean and Colombian rhythms performed with electronic instruments. A generic term used to explain the ethnic blending of urban Peruvian society.

*chifa*: A generic term defining Peruvian cuisine of Chinese origin. Chinese restaurants are also referred to as *chifas*.

*cholo*: A term used to refer to a mestizo.

*comida criolla*: A generic term defining the coastal cuisine of Peru.

*corregidor*: A crown envoy who administered the proper use of Indian labor in the Spanish colonies.

*Costumbrismo*: A form of literature written in the nineteenth century portraying local customs and social behavior.

*coya*: The main wife of the Inca. Sometimes, she was also his sister.

*criollo*: A term used to refer to an individual who is the offspring of Spanish parents, born in Peru. In a more general sense it refers to the coastal culture of Peru.

*departmento*: The main political and geographic division of Peru. Departments are the equivalent of a state in the United States.

*el oncenio*: The eleven-year administration of President Augusto B. Leguía between 1919–1929.

*Enlightenment*: A philosophical movement that originated in France in the eighteenth century. The thinkers of the Enlightenment believed in the power of reason and the criticism of traditional institutions such as the monarchy and the Church.

*festejo*: An Afro-Peruvian dance usually performed on the coast of Peru.

*fiesta*: Feast.

*graffito*: A rock surface with an inscription or drawing.

*guano*: A natural fertilizer from bird manure.

*haciendas*: Large farm estates traditionally owned by Peru's ruling elite.

*hidalgo*: A knight. It was the lowest title in Spanish nobility given to an individual by the Spanish crown.

*huayno*: A celebratory dance in the Andes performed by couples. Its music includes the use of violins, harps, flutes, and guitars.

*inti*: Quechua term meaning sun; the main deity of the Inca empire. Also the name of Peruvian currency during the 1980s.

*juane*: A traditional dish in the Amazon basin made of herbs, rice, and chicken, all wrapped in banana leaves.

*junta*: A form of government made up by more than one individual in a military regime.

*limeño*: A native of Lima, Peru's capital.

*maguey*: A form of wood used by Indian sculptors because of its strong fiber.

*marinera*: A festive form of music from the coast. It is performed by couples and features the use of a handkerchief twirled in each dancer's hand.

*mestizaje*: A process that describes the blending of cultures in Peru.

*mestizo*: An individual whose parents or ancestors are of different ethnic origins, especially of Latin American and European ancestry.

*mita*: An ancient form of collective cooperation of the *ayllu*. After the conquest of the Inca empire by the Spanish conquistadors, it was adapted as a form of tax system for Indian labor.

*pachamanca*: A form of cooking in the Andes in which meats and vegetables are cooked underground covered by heated stones.

*panaka*: A corporate group of Incas consisting of all the wives, siblings, and offspring of a former monarch.

*picantería*: A restaurant known for its hot and spicy food.

*picarones*: A donut-shaped dessert made out of pumpkin and served with honey.

*quena*: Andean flute.

*quijada*: A musical instrument of Afro-Peruvian origin made of the jawbone of a donkey or horse.

*retablo*: A wooden craft made by artisans in the highlands to represent a number of popular feasts.

*rondas*: Peasant defense groups.

*semiotic drums*: A wooden Amazonian instrument capable of transmitting messages.

*sol*: A term meaning sun in Spanish. Also the name for Peruvian currency during most of its republican history.

*tercet*: Three lines of verse that rhyme with each other in poetry.

*umsha*: A ceremony performed during the feast of San Juan in the Peruvian Amazon where celebrants dance in couples around a palm tree filled with gifts, trying to bring it down with machete blows.

**viceroy.** The highest representative of the king of Spain in the Spanish colonies. Peru had a total of forty viceroys.

**yaraví.** A form of Andean music and poetry. Its lyrics are usually sad and express loss.

**zampoña.** A pan-pipe Andean instrument.

**zarzuela.** A Spanish form of opera of the nineteenth century.

# Selected Bibliography

Adorno, Rolena. *Guamán Poma: Writing and Resistance in Colonial Peru*. Austin: University of Texas Press, 2000.

Alberti, Giorgio, and Enrique Mayer, eds. *Reciprocidad e intercambio en los Andes Peruanos*. Lima: Instituto de Estudios Peruanos, 1974.

Alden Mason, J. *The Ancient Civilisations of Peru*. New York: Penguin Books, 1957.

Altamirano, Teófilo. *Exodo: Peruanos en el Exterior*. Lima: Fondo Editorial Pontificia Universidad Católica del Perú, 1992.

———. *Liderazgo y organizaciones de peruanos en el exterior*. Lima: PromPeru-Fondo Editorial Pontificia Universidad Católica del Perú, 2000.

Alva, Walter, and Christopher B. Donnan. *Tumbas reales de Sipán. Ceramics of Ancient Peru*. Los Angeles: Fowler Museum of Cultural History, 1993.

Americas Watch. *Peru Under Fire: Human Rights Since the Return to Democracy*. New Haven, CT: Yale University Press, 1992.

Andrien, Kenneth. *Crisis and Decline: The Viceroyalty of Peru in the Seventeenth Century*. Albuquerque: University of New Mexico Press, 1995.

Andrien, Kenneth J., and Rolena Adorno, eds. *Transatlantic Encounters: Europeans and Andeans in the Sixteenth Century*. Berkeley and Los Angeles: University of California Press, 1991.

Balbi, Mariela. *Sato's Cooking Nikkei-Style, Fish and Seafood*. Lima: Universidad de San Martín de Porres, 1997.

Basadre, Jorge. *Historia de la república del Perú*. Lima: Editorial Universitaria, 1968–1969.

Bauer, Brian. *The Development of the Inca State*. Austin: University of Texas Press, 1992.

Bedoya, Ricardo. *Cien años de cine en el Perú*. Lima: Universidad de Lima, Fondo de Desarrollo Editorial-ICI, 1992.

———. *Un cine reencontrado*. Lima: Universidad de Lima, Fondo de Desarrollo Editorial, 1997.

Booth, David, and Bernardo Sorj, eds. *Military Reformism and Social Classes: The Peruvian Experience, 1968–1980*. New York: St. Martin's Press, 1984.

Bowen, Sally. *The Fujimori File: Peru and Its President 1990–2000*. Lima: Peru Monitor, 2000.

Burga, Manuel, and Alberto Flores Galindo. *Apogeo y crisis de la República Aristocrática*. Lima: Ediciones Rikchay Perú, 1984.

Cadena, Marisol de la. *Indigenous Mestizos: The Politics of Race and Culture in Cuzco, Peru, 1919–1991*. Durham, NC: Duke University Press, 2000.

Cameron, Maxwell. *Democracy and Authoritarianism in Peru: Political Coalitions and Social Change*. New York: St. Martin's Press, 1994.

Carcedo, Paloma, Eduardo Dargent, Felipe de Lucio, and Eduardo Wuffarden. *The Silver and Silversmiths of Peru*. Lima: Patronato de Plata del Perú.

Contreras, Carlos, and Marcos Cueto. *Historia del Perú contemporáneo*. Lima: Red para el Desarrollo de las Ciencias Sociales en el Perú, 1999.

Cook, Noble David. *Demographic Collapse: Indian Peru, 1520–1620*. Cambridge: Cambridge University Press, 1981.

Crabtree, John, and Jim Thomas, eds. *Fujimori's Peru: The Political Economy*. London: Institute of Latin American Studies, 1998.

Custer, Felipe Antonio. *The Art of Peruvian Cuisine*. Lima: Ediciones Ganesha. 2000.

Degregori, Carlos Iván. *El nacimiento de Sendero Luminoso*. Lima: Instituto de Estudios Peruanos, 1990.

De Soto, Hernando. *The Other Path: The Invisible Revolution in the Third World*. New York: Harper and Row, 1990.

Del Busto, José Antonio. *Francisco Pizarro, El Marqués Gobernador*. Lima: Editorial Brasa, 1993.

Donnan, Christopher. *Ceramics of Ancient Peru*. Los Angeles: Fowler Museum of Cultural History, 1992.

Fisher, John R. *Silver Mines and Silver Miners in Colonial Peru, 1776–1824*. Liverpool: University of Liverpool, 1977.

Fleet, Michael, and Brian H. Smith. *The Catholic Church and Democracy in Chile and Peru*. Notre Dame, IN: University of Notre Dame Press, 1997.

Flores Galindo, Alberto. *Buscando un inca: Identidad y utopía en los Andes*. Lima: Instituto de Apoyo Agrario, 1987.

Foster, David William. *Peruvian Literature: A Bibliography of Secondary Sources*. Westport, CT: Greenwood, 1981.

Gerdes, Dick. *Mario Vargas Llosa*. Boston: Twayne Publishers, 1985.

Gorriti, Gustavo. *The Shining Path: A History of the Millenarian War in Peru*. Chapel Hill: University of North Carolina Press, 1999.

Guidoni, Enrico, and Roberto Magni. *Monuments of Civilization: The Andes*. New York: Grosset and Dunlap, 1977.

Gunther Doering, Juan, and Guillermo Lohmann Villena. *Lima*. Madrid: Editorial Mapfre, 1992.

Gutiérrez, Gustavo. *A Theology of Liberation: History, Politics, and Salvation*. New York: Orbis Books, 1988.

Hemming, John. *The Conquest of the Incas*. London: Book Club Associates, 1973.

Higgins, James. *A History of Peruvian Literature*. Liverpool, England: Francis Cairns Publications, 1987.

Hudson, Rex, ed. *Peru: A Country Study*. Washington, DC: Library of Congress, 1993.

Kimura, Rei. *Alberto Fujimori of Peru: The President Who Dared to Dream*. New York: Beekman Pub., 1988.

Klaiber, S. J. Jeffrey. *The Catholic Church in Peru, 1821–1985: A Social History*. Washington, DC: Catholic University of America Press, 1992.

Klarén, Peter. *Peru: Society and Nationhood in the Andes*. New York: Oxford University Press, 2000.

Lockhart, James. *The Men of Cajamarca*. Austin: University of Texas Press, 1972.

Malpass, Michael A. *Daily Life in the Inca Empire*. Westport, CT: Greenwood Press, 1996.

Mariátegui. José Carlos. *Seven Interpretive Essays on Peruvian Reality*. Austin: University of Texas Press, 1985.

Markham, Sir Clements R. *The Incas of Peru*. Lima: Librerías ABC, 1969.

Masterson, Daniel M. *Militarism and Politics in Latin America: Peru from Sánchez Cerro to Sendero Luminoso*. Westport, CT: Greenwood Press, 1991.

Matos Mar, José. *Desborde popular: El nuevo rostro del Perú en la década de 1980*. Lima: Instituto de Estudios Peruanos, 1984.

McGregor, S. J. Felipe. *Violence in the Andean Region*. Assen, the Netherlands: Van Gorcum, 1993.

Métaux, Alfred. *The History of the Incas*. New York: Schoken Books, 1961.

Morris, Craig, and Adriana von Hagen. *The Inka Empire and Its Andean Origins*. New York: American Museum of Natural History and Abbeville Press, 1993.

Morris, Robert J. *The Contemporary Peruvian Theatre*. Lubbock: Texas Tech University Press, 1977.

Moseley, Michael E. *The Incas and Their Ancestors: The Archaeology of Peru*. London: Thames & Hudson, 1993.

Ossio, Juan. *Ideología mesiánica del mundo andino: Antología*. Lima: Ignacio Prado Pastor, 1973.

Palmer, David Scott. *The Shining Path of Peru*. New York: St. Martin's Press, 1992.

Pease, Franklin. *Breve historia contemporánea del Perú*. Mexico: Fondo de Cultura Económica, 1995.

———. *Los crónicas y los Andes*. Lima: Fondo de Cultura Económica, 1995.

Peña, Margarita. *Theologies and Liberation in Peru: The Role of Ideas in Social Movements*. Philadelphia, PA: Temple University Press, 1995.

Poole, Deborah, and Gerardo Rénique. *Peru: Time of Fear*. London and New York: Latin American Bureau, Monthly Review Press, 1992.

Portocarrero, Gonzalo, ed. *Los nuevos limeños*. Lima: Sur-Casa de Estudios del Socialismo, 1993.

Prescott, William H. *History of the Conquest of Peru*. New York: Modern Library, 1936.

Read, Jan. *The New Conquistadors*. London: Evans Brothers, 1980.

Rostorowski de Diez Canseco, María. *History of the Inca Realm*. Cambridge: Cambridge University Press, 1998.

Seligman, Linda J. *Between Reform and Revolution: Political Struggles in the Peruvian Andes, 1969–1991*. Stanford, CA: Stanford University Press, 1995.

Sempat Assadourian, Carlos. *El sistema de la economía colonial: Mercado interno, regiones y espacio económico*. Lima: Instituto de Estudios Peruanos, 1981.

Someda, Hidefuji. *El imperio de los Incas: Imagen del Tahuantinsuyo creada por los cronistas*. Lima: Fondo Editorial Pontificia Universidad Católica del Perú, 1999.

Soto, Hernando de. *The Other Path: The Invisible Revolution in the Third World*. New York: Harper & Row, 1989.

Spalding, Karen Williams. *De indio a campesino: Cambios en la estructura social del Perú Colonial*. Lima: Instituto de Estudios Peruanos, 1974.

Starn, Orin, Carlos Iván Degregori, and Robin Kirk, eds. *The Peru Reader: History, Culture, Politics*. Durham, NC: Duke University Press, 1995.

Stokes, Susan. *Cultures in Conflict: Social Movements and the State in Peru*. Berkeley and Los Angeles: University of California Press, 1995.

Thorp, Rosemary and Geoffrey Bertram. *Peru 1890–1977: Growth and Policy in an Open Economy*. New York: Columbia University Press, 1978.

Tulchin, Joseph, and Gary Bland, eds. *Peru in Crisis: Dictatorship or Democracy?* Boulder, CO: Lynne Rienner Publishers and the Woodrow Wilson Center, 1994.

Vargas Llosa, Mario. *A Fish in the Water: A Memoir*. New York: Farrar Straus Giroux, 1994.

Vega, Garcilaso de la. *Royal Commentary of the Incas and General History of Peru*. Austin: University of Texas Press, 1966.

Vich, Víctor. *El discurso de la calle: los cómicos ambulantes y las tensiones de la modernidad en el Peru*. Lima: Red Para el Desarrollo de las Ciencias Sociales en el Perú, 2001.

Wachtel, Nathan. *The Vision of the Vanquished: The Spanish Conquest of Peru Through Indian Eyes*. New York: Barnes and Noble, 1977.

Werlich, David P. *Peru: A Short History*. Carbondale: Southern Illinois University Press, 1978.

Youngers, Coletta A. *Deconstructing Democracy: Peru Under President Alberto Fujimori*. Washington, DC: Washington Office on Latin America, 2000.

Zuidema, R. Thomas. *Inca Civilization in Cuzco*. Austin: University of Texas Press, 1990.

# Index

Agurto de Olaya, Luis, 143
Alegría, Alonso, 117
Alegría, Ciro, 89, 90
Alianza Popular Revolucionaria Americana (APRA), 24–30, 32, 63, 64, 66, 67, 69
Amaru, Túpac (Condorcanqui, José Gabriel), 21, 79, 84, 112
Arguedas, José María, 40, 89, 90, 91, 92, 120
Ascensio Segura, Manuel, 85, 114
Atahualpa, 14, 15, 17, 18, 19, 53

Baca, Susana, 125
Baca Flor, Carlos, 133
Balta, José, 23, 62
Bayly, Jaime, 99, 111
Belaúnde, Fernando, 26, 27, 28, 29, 63, 65, 68
Belaúnde, Víctor Andrés, 87
Belli, Carlos Germán, 100, 101
Benavides, Oscar R., 25, 66
Bingham, Hiram, 144–145
Bolívar, Simón, 22, 61, 84, 132, 142
Bryce Echenique, Alfredo, 93, 95, 96, 98

Bullfighting, 40, 43, 113, 132, 146
Bustamante y Rivero, José Luis, 26, 67

Cabello de Carbonera, Mercedes, 86
Caffa, Melchor, 141
Camino Brent, Enrique, 135
Cápac, Huayna, 15, 16, 17
Cápac, Manco, 12, 78, 142
Carrió de la Vandera, Alonso (Concolorcorvo), 82
Castilla, Ramón, 22–23, 142
Centeno de Osma, Gabriel, 78, 113
Cerpa, Néstor, 30
Chambi, Martín, 144–145
Chavín, 9, 11, 112, 136
Chocano, José Santos, 87
Cisneros, Antonio, 101, 102
*Correo*, 69
Courret, Eugene and Aquiles, 144

Domínguez, Carlos, 145

Eguren, José María, 87, 101
*El Comercio*, 25, 62–63, 64, 73
*El Peruano*, 61, 70
*El Tiempo*, 64, 66

Espinosa Medrano, Juan (El Lunarejo), 78, 113
Expreso, 67–69

Fierro, Pancho, 132–133
Fujimori, Alberto, 29, 30, 31, 37, 41, 69, 74, 98, 120

García, Alan, 25, 28, 29, 32
García Calderón, Ventura, 87
Garrido Lecca, Celso, 124
Gavilán, Baltazar, 141
Gil de Castro, José, 132
González, Miki, 127
González Prada, Manuel, 85, 86
Goldemberg, Isaac, 98, 99
Granda, Chabuca, 124
Grau, Ricardo, 134, 135
Gutiérrez, Gustavo, 40
Gutiérrez, Sérvulo 134–135
Guzmán, Abimael, 28, 29, 120

*Hablemos de cine*, 108
Hare, Billy, 145–146, 147
Haya de la Torre, Víctor Raúl, 24, 25, 26, 27, 28, 63, 66, 67, 143
Heraud, Javier, 101
Hernández, Daniel, 134
Hernández, Luis, 101
Holy Week (Semana Santa), 38, 44
Huáscar, 14, 15, 16, 17, 19
Huarcaya, Roberto, 147
Humboldt, Alexander von, 4

Inca empire, 1, 8, 12–17, 18, 51, 53, 77, 78, 112, 122, 142
Independientes, 134, 135
*Indianismo* (Indianism), 89
*Indigenismo* (Indigenism, Indigenist Movement), 88–91, 134–136
Inquisition, 20–21, 38

*La Crónica*, 65
*La Gaceta de Lima*, 61

*La Prensa*, 63–65, 67, 69, 109
*La Razón*, 66
*La República*, 69–70
La Rosa, Fernando, 146–147
*La Tribuna*, 66–67
Laso, Francisco, 133
Leguía, Augusto B., 24, 25, 28, 62, 63, 64, 66, 70, 142
Liberation Theology, 40
Lombardi, Francisco, 109, 111–112

Machu Picchu, 136, 144
Mariátegui, José Carlos, 24, 25, 64, 66, 88–89, 143
Martínez, Gregorio, 99
Matto de Turner, Clorinda, 86, 89
Meiggs, Henry, 23
*Mercurio Peruano*, 61, 84
Merino, Ignacio, 133
*Mestizaje*, 41, 49–52, 53, 54, 55
Montesinos, Vladimiro, 30, 32
Morales Bermúdez, Francisco, 27, 63, 65, 69
Movimiento Revolucionario Túpac Amaru (MRTA), 28, 30, 119

Noguera, Pedro, 140, 141
Núñez de Vela, Blasco, 20

Ocaña, Artemio, 143
Odría, Manuel A., 26, 64, 67, 95
*Ollantay*, 78, 79, 113

Palma, Ricardo, 76, 85, 86, 117
Paniagua, Valentín, 32
Pardo, José, 66
Pardo, Manuel, 23, 62
Pardo y Aliaga, Felipe, 85, 114
Pérez de Cuéllar, Javier, 30
Piérola, Nicolás de, 24, 62, 66
Pinglo Alva, Felipe, 124
Pisco, 58
Pizarro, Francisco, 1, 16, 18–20, 37, 38, 53, 79, 80

Prado, Manuel, 25, 26, 64, 65, 66, 67, 107
Protestantism, 40, 41

Qoyllur Riti (The Lord of Snow), 44, 45

Retablos, 41
Ribeyro, Julio Ramón, 92, 93, 95, 96, 97, 117, 120
Riva Agüero, José de la, 87
Robles, Daniel Alomía, 124
Robles Godoy, Armando, 109–111

Sabogal, José, 134
Salazar Bondy, Sebastián, 92, 114–116
San Juan (The Festival of St. John), 46
San Martín, José de, 21, 22, 132, 142
San Martín de Porras, 40
Sánchez Cerro, Luis, 25, 63, 66
Santa Rosa de Lima, 40, 113
Scorza, Manuel, 91
Señor de los Milagros (Lord of Miracles), 39, 42, 43
Señor de Qoyllur Riti (The Lord of Snow), 44–45
Silva Meinel, Javier, 146

Sologuren, Javier, 100
Shining Path (Sendero Luminoso), 28, 29, 102, 111, 119, 120
Suárez-Vértiz, Pedro, 127
Szyszlo, Fernando de, 135

Tahuantinsuyo, 13, 15. *See also* Inca empire
Toledo, Alejandro, 31, 32
Toledo, Francisco, 20

*Ultima Hora,* 67
Unanue, Hipólito, 21, 61
Universidad Mayor de San Marcos (San Marcos University), 79, 84, 90, 114

Vallejo, César, 88
Varela, Blanca, 100, 101
Vargas Llosa, Mario, 29, 41, 93, 94, 95, 96, 97, 98, 111, 112, 119, 120
Vega, El Inca Garcilaso de la, 80–82, 112
Velasco Alvarado, Juan, 4, 6, 27, 63, 64, 65, 67, 68, 69, 74, 108, 118
Virgen de la Candelaria, 45–46
Viscardo y Guzmán, Juan Pablo, 21, 84

## About the Authors

CÉSAR FERREIRA is Associate Professor of Spanish at the University of Oklahoma.

EDUARDO DARGENT-CHAMOT is Associate Professor of History at the University of Lima, Peru.